Math Expressions

Homework and Remembering • Volume 1

Developed by
The Children's Math Worlds Research Project

PROJECT DIRECTOR AND AUTHOR
Dr. Karen C. Fuson

This material is based upon work supported by the
National Science Foundation
under Grant Numbers
ESI-9816320, REC-9806020, and RED-935373.

Any opinions, findings, and conclusions, or recommendations expressed in this material
are those of the author and do not necessarily reflect the views of the National Science Foundation.

HOUGHTON MIFFLIN HARCOURT

Teacher Reviewers

Kindergarten
Patricia Stroh Sugiyama
Wilmette, Illinois

Barbara Wahle
Evanston, Illinois

Grade 1
Sandra Budson
Newton, Massachusetts

Janet Pecci
Chicago, Illinois

Megan Rees
Chicago, Illinois

Grade 2
Molly Dunn
Danvers, Massachusetts

Agnes Lesnick
Hillside, Illinois

Rita Soto
Chicago, Illinois

Grade 3
Jane Curran
Honesdale, Pennsylvania

Sandra Tucker
Chicago, Illinois

Grade 4
Sara Stoneberg Llibre
Chicago, Illinois

Sheri Roedel
Chicago, Illinois

Grade 5
Todd Atler
Chicago, Illinois

Leah Barry
Norfolk, Massachusetts

Credits

Cover art: (t) © Superstock/Alamy
Illustrative art: Dave Klug
Technical art: Morgan-Cain & Associates

Study Plan

1. On this hundred grid, dark segments have been drawn separating groups of 9, and the 9s count-bys have been circled. Describe three patterns you see.

1	11	21	31	41	51	61	71	(81)	91
2	12	22	32	42	52	62	(72)	82	92
3	13	23	33	43	53	(63)	73	83	93
4	14	24	34	44	(54)	64	74	84	94
5	15	25	35	(45)	55	65	75	85	95
6	16	26	(36)	46	56	66	76	86	96
7	17	(27)	37	47	57	67	77	87	97
8	(18)	28	38	48	58	68	78	88	98
(9)	19	29	39	49	59	69	79	89	99
10	20	30	40	50	60	70	80	(90)	100

_____

_____

_____

_____

2. Using words or drawings, tell how you remember the 9s multiplications and divisions.

_____

_____

_____

Solve each problem.

3. Kristin's apartment building has 3 floors. Each floor has 9 apartments. How many apartments are there in Kristin's building?

_____

4. Maria has 6 piles of flash cards. If there are 9 cards in each pile, how many flash cards does Maria have in all?

_____

Remembering

Solve. Circle any that you did not know right away so you can practice them more.

1. 2 • 1 = ___   **2.** 2 * 10 = ___   **3.** 2 • 6 = ___   **4.** 5 * 7 = ___

5. 5 × 8 = ___   **6.** 5 × 3 = ___   **7.** 2 × 8 = ___   **8.** 2 × 9 = ___

9. 5 * 2 = ___   **10.** 2 • 5 = ___   **11.** 5 * 1 = ___   **12.** 2 • 3 = ___

13. 2 × 7 = ___   **14.** 5 × 6 = ___   **15.** 2 × 4 = ___   **16.** 5 × 4 = ___

17. 5 • 5 = ___   **18.** 2 * 2 = ___   **19.** 5 • 9 = ___   **20.** 5 * 10 = ___

21. 5 ÷ 5 = ___   **22.** 6 / 2 = ___   **23.** $2\overline{)12}$ **24.** $\frac{8}{2}$ = ___

25. $2\overline{)20}$ **26.** 10 ÷ 5 = ___   **27.** $\frac{18}{2}$ = ___   **28.** $5\overline{)30}$

29. $\frac{40}{5}$ = ___   **30.** $2\overline{)2}$ **31.** 35 ÷ 5 = ___   **32.** 4 / 2 = ___

33. 14 ÷ 2 = ___   **34.** $\frac{20}{5}$ = ___   **35.** $5\overline{)15}$ **36.** 45 ÷ 5 = ___

37. $5\overline{)25}$ **38.** 10 ÷ 2 = ___   **39.** 50 / 5 = ___   **40.** $2\overline{)16}$

Solve each problem.

41. Penelope has 6 apples. She ate 2 of them. How many apples does she have now?

_____

42. Maurice has 6 pairs of shoes to polish. He polishes 5 shoes. How many does he have to polish now?

_____

43. Write and solve an addition or subtraction word problem.

_____

_____

_____

_____

Patterns in 2s, 5s, 10s, and 9s

Homework

Study Plan

1. Write two multiplication equations to represent this array.

   _____

   _____

   ★ ★ ★ ★ ★ ★
   ★ ★ ★ ★ ★ ★
   ★ ★ ★ ★ ★ ★
   ★ ★ ★ ★ ★ ★
   ★ ★ ★ ★ ★ ★

Make a math drawing for each problem and then solve.

2. Mr. Jones has a small orchard in his backyard. His orchard has 8 rows of apple trees. Each row has 5 trees. How many apple trees are in his orchard?

3. The teachers' parking lot has 3 rows of parking spaces with the same number of spaces in each row. If 27 cars can park in the lot, many spaces are in each row?

4. On a separate sheet of paper, write and solve an array multiplication problem.

5. **Math Journal** Explain how you know that multiplication is commutative.

Use your Target to practice. Focus on the multiplications and divisions in your Study Plan.

Remembering

Solve.

1. $9 \cdot 1 =$ ___   **2.** $9 * 10 =$ ___   **3.** $9 \cdot 6 =$ ___   **4.** $10 * 7 =$ ___

5. $10 \times 8 =$ ___   **6.** $10 \times 3 =$ ___   **7.** $9 \times 8 =$ ___   **8.** $9 \times 9 =$ ___

9. $10 * 2 =$ ___   **10.** $9 \cdot 5 =$ ___   **11.** $10 * 1 =$ ___   **12.** $9 \cdot 3 =$ ___

13. $9 \times 7 =$ ___   **14.** $10 \times 6 =$ ___   **15.** $9 \times 4 =$ ___   **16.** $10 \times 4 =$ ___

17. $10 \cdot 5 =$ ___   **18.** $9 * 2 =$ ___   **19.** $10 \cdot 9 =$ ___   **20.** $10 * 10 =$ ___

21. $10 \div 10 =$ ___   **22.** $\frac{27}{9} =$ ___   **23.** $9\overline{)54}$ **24.** $36 \div 9 =$ ___

25. $9\overline{)90}$ **26.** $20 \div 10 =$ ___   **27.** $70 / 10 =$ ___   **28.** $10\overline{)60}$

29. $\frac{40}{10} =$ ___   **30.** $9\overline{)9}$ **31.** $81 \div 9 =$ ___   **32.** $\frac{18}{9} =$ ___

33. $63 \div 9 =$ ___   **34.** $80 \div 10 =$ ___   **35.** $10\overline{)30}$ **36.** $90 \div 10 =$ ___

37. $10\overline{)50}$ **38.** $45 \div 9 =$ ___   **39.** $100 / 10 =$ ___   **40.** $9\overline{)72}$

Solve each problem.

41. One day at the pond, Allie caught 12 tadpoles. Mark only caught 6 tadpoles. How many more tadpoles did Allie catch?

_____

42. Jasper knew how to cook 9 recipes. Then he learned 3 more. How many recipes does Jasper know how to cook now?

_____

43. Write and solve an addition or subtraction word problem.

_____

_____

_____

_____

_____

Arrays and Commutativity

Study Plan

Write a multiplication equation to represent the total.

1. How many eggs?

_____

2. How many legs?

_____

3. How many basketballs?

_____

4. How many points?

_____

5. Complete this table.

Rabbits r	r	3	7	9		8	6		400
Ears $2 \cdot r$	e	2			10	8		80	2,000

6. On a separate sheet of paper, write a division word problem involving groups in which the group size is unknown. Write your solution underneath the problem.

Name _Mya (7)_   Date _____

Remembering

Multiply.

1. 4 • 5 = _20_   **2.** 8 * 2 = _16_   **3.** 9 • 5 = _45_   **4.** 7 * 2 = _14_

5. 3 × 2 = _6_   **6.** 3 × 10 = _30_   **7.** 1 × 2 = _2_   **8.** 9 × 9 = _81_

9. 4 * 9 = _36_   **10.** 2 • 9 = _18_   **11.** 6 * 9 = _54_   **12.** 3 • 5 = _15_

13. 10 × 2 = _20_   **14.** 5 × 5 = _25_   **15.** 2 × 5 = _10_   **16.** 1 × 9 = _9_

17. 8 • 9 = _72_   **18.** 4 * 2 = _8_   **19.** 10 • 9 = _90_   **20.** 2 * 2 = _4_

21. 7 × 5 = _35_   **22.** 8 × 5 = _40_   **23.** 6 × 2 = _12_   **24.** 6 × 5 = _30_

25. 8 * 10 = _80_   **26.** 7 • 9 = _63_   **27.** 3 * 9 = _27_   **28.** 5 • 9 = _45_

29. 5 • 2 = _10_   **30.** 1 * 5 = _5_   **31.** 10 • 5 = _50_   **32.** 9 * 2 = _18_

Solve each problem.

33. Larry has 35 nuts. Seven are almonds and the rest are walnuts. How many are walnuts?

5 walnuts _____

34. Flora planted 4 tulips and 12 snapdragons. How many flowers did she plant?

12+4=16 flowers _____

35. On a separate sheet of paper, write a division word problem involving groups in which the number of groups (the multiplier) is unknown. Then solve it.

Cut out the product cards on pages 9, 10, 11 and 12. Practice your multiplications and divisions using the Product Cards and your Target.

2×2

$2 \cdot 3$

Hint:
What is $3 \cdot 2$?

$2 * 4$

Hint:
What is $4 * 2$?

2×5

Hint:
What is 5×2?

2×6

Hint:
What is 6×2?

$2 \cdot 7$

Hint:
What is $7 \cdot 2$?

$2 * 8$

Hint:
What is $8 * 2$?

2×9

Hint:
What is 9×2?

5×2

Hint:
What is 2×5?

$5 \cdot 3$

Hint:
What is $3 \cdot 5$?

$5 * 4$

Hint:
What is $4 * 5$?

5×5

5×6

Hint:
What is 6×5?

$5 \cdot 7$

Hint:
What is $7 \cdot 5$?

$5 * 8$

Hint:
What is $8 * 5$?

5×9

Hint:
What is 9×5?

Product Cards: 2s, 5s, 9s

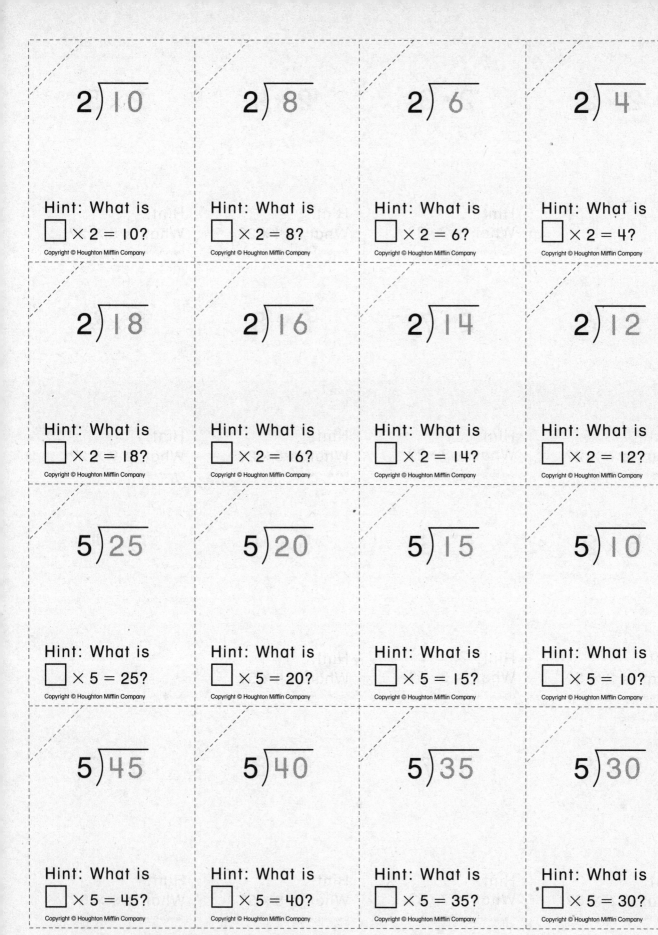

$2\overline{)10}$

Hint: What is
$\square \times 2 = 10$?

$2\overline{)8}$

Hint: What is
$\square \times 2 = 8$?

$2\overline{)6}$

Hint: What is
$\square \times 2 = 6$?

$2\overline{)4}$

Hint: What is
$\square \times 2 = 4$?

$2\overline{)18}$

Hint: What is
$\square \times 2 = 18$?

$2\overline{)16}$

Hint: What is
$\square \times 2 = 16$?

$2\overline{)14}$

Hint: What is
$\square \times 2 = 14$?

$2\overline{)12}$

Hint: What is
$\square \times 2 = 12$?

$5\overline{)25}$

Hint: What is
$\square \times 5 = 25$?

$5\overline{)20}$

Hint: What is
$\square \times 5 = 20$?

$5\overline{)15}$

Hint: What is
$\square \times 5 = 15$?

$5\overline{)10}$

Hint: What is
$\square \times 5 = 10$?

$5\overline{)45}$

Hint: What is
$\square \times 5 = 45$?

$5\overline{)40}$

Hint: What is
$\square \times 5 = 40$?

$5\overline{)35}$

Hint: What is
$\square \times 5 = 35$?

$5\overline{)30}$

Hint: What is
$\square \times 5 = 30$?

Product Cards: 2s, 5s, 9s

9×2

$9 \cdot 3$

$9 * 4$

9×5

Hint:
What is 2×9?

Hint:
What is $3 \cdot 9$?

Hint:
What is $4 * 9$?

Hint:
What is 5×9?

9×6

$9 \cdot 7$

$9 * 8$

9×9

Hint:
What is 6×9?

Hint:
What is $7 \cdot 9$?

Hint:
What is $8 * 9$?

$\times$

$\cdot$

$*$

$\times$

$\times$

$\cdot$

$*$

$\times$

You can write any numbers on the last 8 cards. Use them to practice difficult problems or if you lose a card.

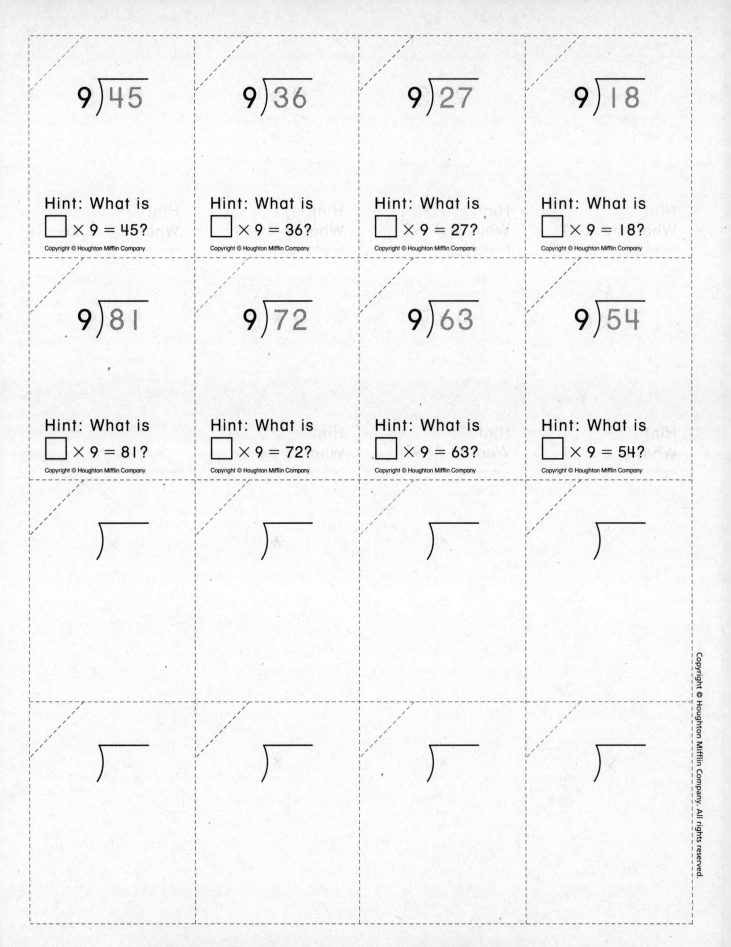

$9\overline{)45}$

Hint: What is
$\square \times 9 = 45$?

$9\overline{)36}$

Hint: What is
$\square \times 9 = 36$?

$9\overline{)27}$

Hint: What is
$\square \times 9 = 27$?

$9\overline{)18}$

Hint: What is
$\square \times 9 = 18$?

$9\overline{)81}$

Hint: What is
$\square \times 9 = 81$?

$9\overline{)72}$

Hint: What is
$\square \times 9 = 72$?

$9\overline{)63}$

Hint: What is
$\square \times 9 = 63$?

$9\overline{)54}$

Hint: What is
$\square \times 9 = 54$?

You can write any numbers on the last 8 cards. Use them to practice difficult problems or if you lose a card.

Product Cards: 2s, 5s, 9s

Homework

Study Plan

1. On a separate sheet of paper, make a table of 10 rows and 3 columns. In your table, copy the multiplication and division equations shown on the right. Then:

1 × 3 = 3	3 ÷ 1 = 3	3 / 3 = 1
2 * 3 = 6	6 / 2 = 3	6 ÷ 3 = 2
3 · 3 = 9		

- Complete the first column by writing equations to show all 3s multiplication up to 10 × 3.

- Complete the second and third columns by writing division equations.

Write a multiplication equation to represent each total.

2. How many bananas?

_____

3. How many holes?

_____

Solve each problem.

4. Mai-Lin has 3 plums for each of her friends. If she has 6 friends, how many plums does she have?

_____

5. Luis has 18 tickets for the carnival. If each ride costs 3 tickets, how many rides can he go on?

_____

Remembering

Divide.

1. $27 \div 9 =$ _____   **2.** $14 \div 2 =$ _____   **3.** $45 \div 5 =$ _____   **4.** $20 \div 5 =$ _____

5. $9\overline{)45}$ **6.** $\dfrac{72}{9} =$ _____   **7.** $54 \div 9 =$ _____   **8.** $63 \div 9 =$ _____

9. $25 \div 5 =$ _____   **10.** $18 \div 9 =$ _____   **11.** $5\overline{)30}$ **12.** $35 / 5 =$ _____

13. $36 / 9 =$ _____   **14.** $90 \div 9 =$ _____   **15.** $81 \div 9 =$ _____   **16.** $80 \div 10 =$ _____

17. $60 \div 10 =$ _____   **18.** $5\overline{)50}$ **19.** $2\overline{)20}$ **20.** $5\overline{)40}$

21. On the grid to the right, dark segments have been drawn separating groups of 3, and the 3s count-bys have been circled. Describe two patterns you see.

_____

_____

_____

_____

Solve each word problem.

22. One day, an animal shelter took in 9 adult cats and 36 kittens. How many new cats did the shelter take in that day?

_____

23. One day, an animal shelter had 27 kittens. A family came and adopted 4 of the kittens. How many kittens were left after that?

_____

24. Complete this table.

Tricycles t	t	2	5			0	4		200	
Wheels 3·t	w	6		9	21			18		300

Homework

Study Plan

Complete each Equal-Shares Drawing and Fast Array. Then
tell whether the number in the box is a factor or the
product.

1.
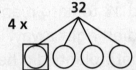

_____

2.
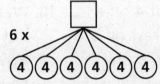

_____

3.
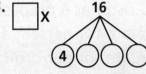

_____

4.
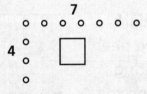

_____

5.
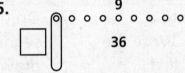

_____

6.

4   24

_____

Use the pictograph to solve each problem.

Animals Treated in June

Animal	Number of Animals
Cat	🥣 🥣 🥣 🥣 🥣 🥣
Dog	🥣 🥣 🥣 🥣 🥣 🥣 🥣 🥣
Reptile	🥣 🥣 🥣
Bird	🥣

🥣 = 10 Animals

7. How many dogs did the veterinarian treat?

_____

8. How many more cats than birds did the veterinarian treat?

_____

Remembering

Solve.

1. $8 \cdot 9 =$ ___   2. $10 \cdot 9 =$ ___   3. $8 * 10 =$ ___   4. $7 \cdot 9 =$ ___

5. $5 \cdot 9 =$ ___   6. $5 \times 5 =$ ___   7. $1 \times 9 =$ ___   8. $4 * 9 =$ ___

9. $6 * 9 =$ ___   10. $3 \cdot 5 =$ ___   11. $5\overline{)30}$ 12. $2\overline{)12}$

13. $27 \div 9 =$ ___   14. $45 \div 5 =$ ___   15. $5\overline{)50}$ 16. $5\overline{)40}$

Solve each problem.

17. Kristi has 8 grapes. She put 4 on a plate for herself, and the rest on a plate for her brother. How many grapes are for her brother?

_____

18. Warren planted 18 tomato plants, but 2 of them died right away. How many tomato plants did he have then?

_____

19. Copy the chart below onto a separate sheet of paper. Write the 4s multiplications in the first column up to 10×4. In the other two columns, write the two divisions you can make from each multiplication. Each column has been started for you.

$1 \times 4 = 4$	$4 \div 1 = 4$	$4/4 = 1$
$2 * 4 = 8$	$8/2 = 4$	$8/4 = 2$
$3 \cdot 4 = 12$		

20. On this grid, dark segments have been drawn separating groups of 4, and the 4s count-bys have been circled. On a separate sheet of paper, describe two patterns you see.

1	11	21	31
2	⓬	22	㉜
3	13	23	33
④	14	㉔	34
5	15	25	35
6	⑯	26	㊱
7	17	27	37
⑧	18	㉘	38
9	19	29	39
10	⑳	30	㊵

21. On a separate sheet of paper, write and solve a 4s multiplication problem and a 4s division problem. One of your problems should be about an array.

Practice multiplications and divisions with the Target and the Product Cards.

Multiply and Divide With 4

Homework

Study Plan

Solve.

1. $0 \cdot 1 =$ ___   **2.** $10 * 0 =$ ___   **3.** $0 \cdot 6 =$ ___   **4.** $1 * 7 =$ ___

5. $1 \cdot 5 =$ ___   **6.** $0 * 2 =$ ___   **7.** $9 * 1 =$ ___   **8.** $1 * 10 =$ ___

9. $1 \div 1 =$ ___   **10.** $3 \div 3 =$ ___   **11.** $6 \div 1 =$ ___   **12.** $5 \div 1 =$ ___

13. $1\overline{)10}$ **14.** $2\overline{)2}$ **15.** $\dfrac{7}{1} =$ ___   **16.** $1\overline{)6}$

17. $\dfrac{4}{4} =$ ___   **18.** $10 / 10 =$ ___   **19.** $\dfrac{9}{1} =$ ___   **20.** $\dfrac{5}{5} =$ ___

21. Math Journal Describe how you remember the 0s and 1s multiplications and divisions.

Use the pictograph to solve each problem.

Brass Instrument Sales	
Instrument	**Number of Sales**
Trombone	𝄞 𝄞 𝄞 𝄞 𝄞 𝄞
French Horn	𝄞 𝄞 𝄞
Tuba	𝄞 𝄞
Trumpet	𝄞 𝄞 𝄞 𝄞 𝄞 𝄞 𝄞 𝄞
	𝄞 = 9 Instruments

22. How many trumpets did the store sell?

_____

23. How many total trombones and tubas did the store sell?

_____

Remembering

Multiply.

1. $7 \cdot 5 =$ _____   2. $5 * 3 =$ _____   3. $1 \cdot 9 =$ _____   4. $9 * 3 =$ _____

5. $1 \times 1 =$ _____   6. $1 \times 10 =$ _____   7. $6 \times 10 =$ _____   8. $8 \times 2 =$ _____

9. $4 * 9 =$ _____   10. $2 \cdot 0 =$ _____   11. $8 * 9 =$ _____   12. $10 \cdot 9 =$ _____

13. $3 \times 2 =$ _____   14. $10 \times 4 =$ _____   15. $5 \times 1 =$ _____   16. $6 \times 4 =$ _____

17. $7 \cdot 10 =$ _____   18. $0 * 3 =$ _____   19. $4 \cdot 5 =$ _____   20. $8 * 0 =$ _____

21. $2 \times 4 =$ _____   22. $6 \times 2 =$ _____   23. $1 \times 3 =$ _____   24. $9 \times 1 =$ _____

Solve each problem.

25. Jude had a package of 15 pencils. He gave 6 to his friend at school. How many pencils did he have left?

_____

26. Sam had 19 toy cars in his collection. Then he received 4 more toy cars for his birthday. How many toy cars does he have altogether?

_____

27. Write and solve an addition or subtraction word problem.

_____

_____

_____

_____

28. Complete the table.

Triangles t	t	6		1		4		20
Sides $3 \cdot t$	s		27		0		15	900

Multiply and Divide With 1 and 0

Homework

Study Plan

Solve each problem.

1. Lou arranged 12 cans in an array with 4 columns. How many rows were in the array?

   _____

2. Pedro's family is moving. Pedro packed his model cars in 7 boxes. He put 3 cars in each box. How many model cars did he pack?

   _____

3. Pedro's little sister packed 36 beanbag animals. She put 9 animals in each box. How many boxes did she use?

   _____

4. At Ramesh's piano recital, the chairs in the audience were set up in 9 rows with 6 chairs in each row. How many chairs were set up?

   _____

5. Complete the table.

Horses h	h	3		0		7		5	300	
Legs $4 \cdot h$	l		24		4		36			8,000

6. On a separate sheet of paper, write and solve a multiplication array problem.

7. On the same sheet you used for problem 6, write and solve a division array problem.

Name _____ **Date** _____

Remembering

Divide.

1. $36 \div 4 =$ ___   **2.** $45 \div 9 =$ ___   **3.** $9\overline{)9}$ **4.** $4\overline{)28}$

5. $\dfrac{100}{10} =$ ___   **6.** $\dfrac{0}{5} =$ ___   **7.** $10 / 1 =$ ___   **8.** $0 \div 1 =$ ___

9. $5\overline{)25}$ **10.** $9\overline{)81}$ **11.** $10 / 5 =$ ___   **12.** $16 / 4 =$ ___

Use this pictograph to solve each problem.

Sandra's Beach Stand Sales

Item	Number of Sales
Sunglasses	☼ ☼
Sunblock	☼ ☼ ☼ ☼ ☼ ☼ ☼ ☼
Sand Pails	☼ ☼ ☼
Inflatable Toys	☼ ☼ ☼ ☼ ☼ ☼

☼ = 3 Items

13. How many inflatable toys did Sandra sell?

_____

14. How many pairs of sunglasses and bottles of sunblock did Sandra sell altogether?

_____

15. How many more inflatable toys did she sell than sand pails?

_____

16. How many pairs of sunglasses and sand pails did Sandra sell in all?

_____

Solve each problem.

17. When Juan went fishing, he saw 18 rainbow trout and 6 speckled trout. How many trout did Juan see in all?

_____

18. A diver has a bucket of 26 fish. She puts 8 fish in a tank. How many fish does she have left?

_____

Fluency Day: 2s, 3s, 4s, 5s, 9s, and 10s

3×2	$3 \cdot 3$	$3 * 4$	3×5
Hint: What is 2×3?	**Hint:**	**Hint:** What is $4 * 3$?	**Hint:** What is 5×3?
3×6	$3 \cdot 7$	$3 * 8$	3×9
Hint: What is 6×3?	**Hint:** What is $7 \cdot 3$?	**Hint:** What is $8 * 3$?	**Hint:** What is 9×3?
4×2	$4 \cdot 3$	$4 * 4$	4×5
Hint: What is 2×4?	**Hint:** What is $3 \cdot 4$?		**Hint:** What is 5×4?
4×6	$4 \cdot 7$	$4 * 8$	4×9
Hint: What is 6×4?	**Hint:** What is $7 \cdot 4$?	**Hint:** What is $8 * 4$?	**Hint:** What is 9×4?

Product Cards: 3s, 4s

$3 \overline{)15}$

Hint: What is
$\square \times 3 = 15?$

$3 \overline{)12}$

Hint: What is
$\square \times 3 = 12?$

$3 \overline{)9}$

Hint: What is
$\square \times 3 = 9?$

$3 \overline{)6}$

Hint: What is
$\square \times 3 = 6?$

$3 \overline{)27}$

Hint: What is
$\square \times 3 = 27?$

$3 \overline{)24}$

Hint: What is
$\square \times 3 = 24?$

$3 \overline{)21}$

Hint: What is
$\square \times 3 = 21?$

$3 \overline{)18}$

Hint: What is
$\square \times 3 = 18?$

$4 \overline{)20}$

Hint: What is
$\square \times 4 = 20?$

$4 \overline{)16}$

Hint: What is
$\square \times 4 = 16?$

$4 \overline{)12}$

Hint: What is
$\square \times 4 = 12?$

$4 \overline{)8}$

Hint: What is
$\square \times 4 = 8?$

$4 \overline{)36}$

Hint: What is
$\square \times 4 = 36?$

$4 \overline{)32}$

Hint: What is
$\square \times 4 = 32?$

$4 \overline{)28}$

Hint: What is
$\square \times 4 = 28?$

$4 \overline{)24}$

Hint: What is
$\square \times 4 = 24?$

Product Cards: 3s, 4s

Homework

Study Plan

---

1. Write eight equations based on this Factor Triangle.

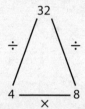

_____   _____

_____   _____

_____   _____

_____   _____

2. Write eight equations based on this Fast Array.

```
   3
  o o o
  o
6 o 18
  o
  o
```

_____   _____

_____   _____

_____   _____

_____   _____

3. Draw a Factor Triangle and a Fast Array for $3 \times 7 = 21$.

4. A nonagon is a closed shape with 9 sides.
Complete this table.

Number of Nonagons n	n	2		4		7		0	100	
Number of Sides $9 \cdot n$	s		54		72		9			2,700

Remembering

Complete each equation.

1. $12 = 3 \times$ ___   2. $8 =$ ___ $\times 4$ 3. ___ $= 3 \times 6$

4. $24 = 4 \times$ ___   5. $35 =$ ___ $\times 5$ 6. ___ $= 8 \times 9$

7. $0 = 5 \times$ ___   8. $9 =$ ___ $\times 3$ 9. ___ $= 4 \times 5$

10. $9 = 1 \times$ ___   11. $36 =$ ___ $\times 4$ 12. ___ $= 5 \times 9$

13. $24 = 3 \times$ ___   14. $0 =$ ___ $\times 9$ 15. ___ $= 4 \times 8$

16. $63 = 9 \times$ ___   17. $21 =$ ___ $\times 3$ 18. ___ $= 3 \times 1$

19. $4 = 20 \div$ ___   20. $4 =$ ___ $\div 10$ 21. ___ $= 4 \div 4$

22. $5 = 25 \div$ ___   23. $5 =$ ___ $\div 3$ 24. ___ $= 40 \div 5$

25. $9 = 54 \div$ ___   26. $0 =$ ___ $\div 9$ 27. ___ $= 28 \div 4$

28. $3 = 12 \div$ ___   29. $9 =$ ___ $\div 2$ 30. ___ $= 24 \div 3$

31. $2 = 6 \div$ ___   32. $0 =$ ___ $\div 3$ 33. ___ $= 7 \div 1$

34. $9 = 36 \div$ ___   35. $4 =$ ___ $\div 4$ 36. ___ $= 32 \div 4$

Solve each problem.

37. Marcus had 20 days to do his science fair project. Maria only had 10 days. How many more days did Marcus have to do his project?

_____

38. The Parents' Club had 6 blueberry muffins and 14 raisin muffins for sale. How many muffins did they have for sale in all?

Related Equations

$$1 \overline{)\ 2} \qquad 1 \overline{)\ 0} \qquad 9 \overline{)\ 4} \qquad 1 \overline{)\ 7} \qquad 8 \overline{)\ 1} \qquad 3 \overline{)\ 3}$$

$$7 \overline{)\ 3} \qquad 7 \overline{)\ 4} \qquad 6 \overline{)\ 0} \qquad 1 \overline{)\ 6} \qquad 1 \overline{)\ 3} \qquad 8 \overline{)\ 0}$$

$$9 \overline{)\ 1} \qquad 5 \overline{)\ 1} \qquad 3 \overline{)\ 5} \qquad 1 \overline{)\ 9} \qquad 3 \overline{)\ 0} \qquad 1 \overline{)\ 10}$$

$$5 \overline{)\ 3} \qquad 6 \overline{)\ 4} \qquad 10 \overline{)\ 0} \qquad 4 \overline{)\ 10} \qquad 5 \overline{)\ 0} \qquad 9 \overline{)\ 3}$$

$$7 \overline{)\ 0} \qquad 3 \overline{)\ 10} \qquad 7 \overline{)\ 1} \qquad 8 \overline{)\ 4} \qquad 10 \overline{)\ 1} \qquad 4 \overline{)\ 8}$$

$$3 \overline{)\ 1} \qquad 2 \overline{)\ 3} \qquad 5 \overline{)\ 4} \qquad 2 \overline{)\ 0} \qquad 10 \overline{)\ 4} \qquad 3 \overline{)\ 7}$$

$$3 \overline{)\ 4} \qquad 4 \overline{)\ 6} \qquad 1 \overline{)\ 5} \qquad 2 \overline{)\ 1} \qquad 3 \overline{)\ 9} \qquad 4 \overline{)\ 4}$$

$$4 \overline{)\ 2} \qquad 1 \overline{)\ 8} \qquad 6 \overline{)\ 1} \qquad 3 \overline{)\ 6} \qquad 2 \overline{)\ 4} \qquad 4 \overline{)\ 1}$$

$$4 \overline{)\ 5} \qquad 10 \overline{)\ 3} \qquad 4 \overline{)\ 7} \qquad 9 \overline{)\ 0} \qquad 4 \overline{)\ 9} \qquad 8 \overline{)\ 3}$$

$$4 \overline{)\ 0} \qquad 1 \overline{)\ 4} \qquad 3 \overline{)\ 8} \qquad 4 \overline{)\ 3} \qquad 3 \overline{)\ 2} \qquad 6 \overline{)\ 3}$$

Name _____

$2\overline{)3}$ $3\overline{)7}$ $8\overline{)4}$ $8\overline{)0}$ $2\overline{)4}$ $6\overline{)3}$

$10\overline{)3}$ $1\overline{)8}$ $1\overline{)0}$ $5\overline{)3}$ $1\overline{)1}$ $4\overline{)4}$

$10\overline{)1}$ $4\overline{)7}$ $7\overline{)4}$ $1\overline{)9}$ $3\overline{)8}$ $1\overline{)7}$

$9\overline{)3}$ $3\overline{)10}$ $1\overline{)5}$ $3\overline{)5}$ $5\overline{)0}$ $6\overline{)0}$

$3\overline{)6}$ $7\overline{)0}$ $6\overline{)4}$ $4\overline{)5}$ $2\overline{)0}$ $6\overline{)1}$

$5\overline{)4}$ $5\overline{)1}$ $10\overline{)4}$ $4\overline{)3}$ $7\overline{)1}$ $4\overline{)1}$

$3\overline{)0}$ $9\overline{)1}$ $10\overline{)0}$ $3\overline{)9}$ $9\overline{)4}$ $4\overline{)10}$

$4\overline{)8}$ $4\overline{)0}$ $3\overline{)1}$ $1\overline{)10}$ $8\overline{)3}$ $3\overline{)3}$

$4\overline{)6}$ $1\overline{)6}$ $3\overline{)4}$ $1\overline{)1}$ $7\overline{)3}$ $3\overline{)2}$

$9\overline{)0}$ $1\overline{)4}$ $4\overline{)2}$ $2\overline{)1}$ $4\overline{)9}$ $8\overline{)1}$

Home Write-On Sheet 1B

2 $1\overline{)2}$	0 $1\overline{)0}$	4 $9\overline{)36}$	7 $1\overline{)7}$	1 $8\overline{)8}$	3 $3\overline{)9}$
3 $7\overline{)21}$	4 $7\overline{)28}$	0 $6\overline{)0}$	6 $1\overline{)6}$	3 $1\overline{)3}$	0 $8\overline{)0}$
1 $9\overline{)9}$	1 $5\overline{)5}$	5 $3\overline{)15}$	9 $1\overline{)9}$	0 $3\overline{)0}$	10 $1\overline{)10}$
3 $5\overline{)15}$	4 $6\overline{)24}$	0 $10\overline{)0}$	10 $4\overline{)40}$	0 $5\overline{)0}$	3 $9\overline{)27}$
0 $7\overline{)0}$	10 $3\overline{)30}$	1 $7\overline{)7}$	4 $8\overline{)32}$	1 $10\overline{)10}$	8 $4\overline{)32}$
1 $3\overline{)3}$	3 $2\overline{)6}$	4 $5\overline{)20}$	0 $2\overline{)0}$	4 $10\overline{)40}$	7 $3\overline{)21}$
4 $3\overline{)12}$	6 $4\overline{)24}$	5 $1\overline{)5}$	1 $2\overline{)2}$	9 $3\overline{)27}$	4 $4\overline{)16}$
2 $4\overline{)8}$	8 $1\overline{)8}$	1 $6\overline{)6}$	6 $3\overline{)18}$	4 $2\overline{)8}$	1 $4\overline{)4}$
5 $4\overline{)20}$	3 $10\overline{)30}$	7 $4\overline{)28}$	0 $9\overline{)0}$	9 $4\overline{)36}$	3 $8\overline{)24}$
0 $4\overline{)0}$	4 $1\overline{)4}$	8 $3\overline{)24}$	3 $4\overline{)12}$	2 $3\overline{)6}$	3 $6\overline{)18}$

Name _____

$2\overline{)6}$ = 3	$3\overline{)21}$ = 7	$8\overline{)32}$ = 4	$8\overline{)0}$ = 0	$2\overline{)8}$ = 4	$6\overline{)18}$ = 3
$10\overline{)30}$ = 3	$1\overline{)8}$ = 8	$1\overline{)0}$ = 0	$5\overline{)15}$ = 3	$1\overline{)1}$ = 1	$4\overline{)16}$ = 4
$10\overline{)10}$ = 1	$4\overline{)28}$ = 7	$7\overline{)28}$ = 4	$1\overline{)9}$ = 9	$3\overline{)24}$ = 8	$1\overline{)7}$ = 7
$9\overline{)27}$ = 3	$3\overline{)30}$ = 10	$1\overline{)5}$ = 5	$3\overline{)15}$ = 5	$5\overline{)0}$ = 0	$6\overline{)0}$ = 0
$3\overline{)18}$ = 6	$7\overline{)0}$ = 0	$6\overline{)24}$ = 4	$4\overline{)20}$ = 5	$2\overline{)0}$ = 0	$6\overline{)6}$ = 1
$5\overline{)20}$ = 4	$5\overline{)5}$ = 1	$10\overline{)40}$ = 4	$4\overline{)12}$ = 3	$7\overline{)7}$ = 1	$4\overline{)4}$ = 1
$3\overline{)0}$ = 0	$9\overline{)9}$ = 1	$10\overline{)0}$ = 0	$3\overline{)27}$ = 9	$9\overline{)36}$ = 4	$4\overline{)40}$ = 10
$4\overline{)32}$ = 8	$4\overline{)0}$ = 0	$3\overline{)3}$ = 1	$1\overline{)1}$ = 10	$8\overline{)24}$ = 3	$3\overline{)9}$ = 3
$4\overline{)24}$ = 6	$1\overline{)6}$ = 6	$3\overline{)12}$ = 4	$1\overline{)1}$ = 1	$7\overline{)21}$ = 3	$3\overline{)6}$ = 2
$9\overline{)0}$ = 0	$1\overline{)4}$ = 4	$4\overline{)8}$ = 2	$2\overline{)2}$ = 1	$4\overline{)36}$ = 9	$8\overline{)8}$ = 1

Home Check Sheet 1B

Name _____ Date _____

Study Plan

Read each problem, decide what type of problem it is, then write the equation and solve.

a. Array Multiplication

b. Array Division

c. Repeated-Groups Multiplication

d. Repeated-Groups Division with Unknown Group Size

e. Repeated-Groups Division with Unknown Multiplier (number of groups)

1. Mother has cooked 1 dozen eggs for breakfast. If there are 6 people in the family, how many eggs can each person have?

Problem Type: _____

Equation: _____

3. A rose garden has 3 rows and 9 bushes in each row. How many rose bushes are there in all?

Problem Type: _____

Equation: _____

2. There are 40 eggs in nests in the park. All of the nests have 5 eggs in them. How many nests are there?

Problem Type: _____

Equation: _____

4. Amelia wrote 2 pages in her journal every night. How many pages did she write each week?

Problem Type: _____

Equation: _____

Name _____ Date _____

Remembering

Solve each problem.

1. A box of oranges has 4 rows. Each row has 8 oranges. How many oranges are in the box?

   _____

2. A classroom has 40 student desks. If there are 5 rows of desks, how many desks are in each row?

   _____

3. Keshawn bought 36 animal stickers for his sisters. He gave 9 stickers to each sister and had none left. How many sisters does he have?

   _____

4. There are 24 students in the school chorus. During their last concert, they stood in 3 equal rows. How many students stood in each row?

   _____

Use a separate sheet of paper for exercises 5 and 6.

5. Write and solve a repeated-groups division problem with unknown group size.

6. Write and solve an array problem.

Use the pictograph to solve each problem.

Art Pieces at a Gallery

Type	Number of Pieces
Drawings	🎨 🎨
Paintings	🎨 🎨 🎨 🎨 🎨 🎨
Sculptures	🎨
Photographs	🎨 🎨 🎨 🎨

🎨 = 9 Pieces

7. How many photographs does the gallery have?

   _____

8. How many more paintings than sculptures does the gallery have?

   _____

9. How many drawings and paintings does the gallery have altogether?

   _____

Homework

Name _____   Date _____

Study Plan

This pictograph shows the number of each type of bagel sold at The Bagel Hut.

1. How many plain bagels were sold?

_____

2. How many wheat and poppy seed bagels were sold altogether?

_____

3. How many more plain bagels were sold than cinnamon raisin bagels?

_____

Number of Bagels Sold

Poppy Seed	🥯 🥯 🥯 🥯
Wheat	🥯 🥯 🥯
Plain	🥯 🥯 🥯 🥯 🥯
Cinnamon Raisin	🥯 🥯

🥯 = 6 bagels

4. On this grid, dark segments have been drawn separating groups of 6, and the 6s count-bys have been circled. Describe two patterns you see.

_____

_____

_____

1	11	21	31	41	51
2	(12)	22	32	(42)	52
3	13	23	33	43	53
4	14	(24)	34	44	(54)
5	15	25	35	45	55
(6)	16	26	(36)	46	56
7	17	27	37	47	57
8	(18)	28	38	(48)	58
9	19	29	39	49	59
10	20	(30)	40	50	(60)

Solve each problem.

5. Thirty-six cars were parked in 6 equal rows. How many cars were parked in each row?

_____

6. Georgia read for 48 minutes. Each page took 8 minutes to read. How many pages did she read?

_____

Remembering

Solve each multiplication and division problem.

1. $5 \cdot 1 =$ ___   **2.** $2 * 3 =$ ___   **3.** $10 \cdot 4 =$ ___   **4.** $5 * 9 =$ ___

5. $4 \times 8 =$ ___   **6.** $3 \times 9 =$ ___   **7.** $7 \times 5 =$ ___   **8.** $8 \times 10 =$ ___

9. $3 \cdot 7 =$ ___   **10.** $5 * 10 =$ ___   **11.** $9 \cdot 2 =$ ___   **12.** $4 * 7 =$ ___

13. $4\overline{)36}$ **14.** $24 \div 3 =$ ___   **15.** $60 / 10 =$ ___   **16.** $6 / 6 =$ ___

17. $30 / 10 =$ ___   **18.** $5\overline{)25}$ **19.** $63 \div 9 =$ ___   **20.** $30 / 5 =$ ___

21. $15 \div 5 =$ ___   **22.** $9 \div 1 =$ ___   **23.** $5\overline{)10}$ **24.** $16 \div 4 =$ ___

25. Write eight equations based on this Addend Triangle.

_____   _____

_____   _____

_____   _____

_____   _____

Solve each problem.

26. George walked 6 blocks to Fred's house. Then he walked 3 more blocks to get to school. How many blocks did George walk in all?

_____

27. Henry had 15 jellybeans. He ate 5 and put the rest away for later. How many jellybeans did he save for later?

_____

Homework

Study Plan

1. Complete this function table.

Weeks w	w	1		4	5		8
Days 7•w	d		21			49	

2. On this grid, dark segments have been drawn separating groups of 8, and the 8s count-bys have been circled. Describe two patterns you see.

1	11	21	31	41	51	61	71
2	12	22	(32)	42	52	62	(72)
3	13	23	33	43	53	63	73
4	14	(24)	34	44	54	(64)	74
5	15	25	35	45	55	65	75
6	(16)	26	36	46	(56)	66	76
7	17	27	37	47	57	67	77
(8)	18	28	38	(48)	58	68	78
9	19	29	39	49	59	69	79
10	20	30	(40)	50	60	70	(80)

_____

_____

_____

_____

Solve each problem.

3. Mei cut a 56-inch piece of yarn into 8-inch pieces. How many pieces does she have?

_____

4. Each box of crayons has 8 crayons. How many crayons are there in 6 boxes?

_____

5. Fiona drinks 3 cups of milk each day. There are 8 ounces of milk in one cup. How many ounces of milk does Fiona drink each day?

_____

6. Bethany is stacking books at her father's bookstore. She has 42 books. She places them in rows of 7. How many books are there in each row?

_____

Name _____   Date _____

Remembering

Solve each multiplication and division problem.

1. $7 \cdot 4 =$ ___   **2.** $0 * 3 =$ ___   **3.** $6 \cdot 5 =$ ___   **4.** $2 * 8 =$ ___

5. $6 \times 1 =$ ___   **6.** $3 \times 9 =$ ___   **7.** $7 \times 0 =$ ___   **8.** $3 \times 10 =$ ___

9. $1 \cdot 9 =$ ___   **10.** $2 * 10 =$ ___   **11.** $7 \cdot 1 =$ ___   **12.** $5 * 0 =$ ___

13. $2 \times 8 =$ ___   **14.** $3 \times 3 =$ ___   **15.** $5 \times 5 =$ ___   **16.** $8 \times 5 =$ ___

17. $5\overline{)45}$ **18.** $32 \div 4 =$ ___   **19.** $24 / 8 =$ ___   **20.** $18 / 6 =$ ___

21. $7 / 7 =$ ___   **22.** $9\overline{)81}$ **23.** $20 \div 4 =$ ___   **24.** $28 / 4 =$ ___

25. $40 \div 5 =$ ___   **26.** $10 \div 10 =$ ___   **27.** $3\overline{)21}$ **28.** $8 \div 8 =$ ___

29. $12 / 4 =$ ___   **30.** $4\overline{)24}$ **31.** $54 \div 9 =$ ___   **32.** $50 / 5 =$ ___

33. $24 / 8 =$ ___   **34.** $9\overline{)63}$ **35.** $35 \div 5 =$ ___   **36.** $9 / 1 =$ ___

Solve each problem.

37. At a dog kennel, 6 puppies were born in the morning and 5 more were born in the afternoon. How many puppies were born altogether?

_____

38. Eileen has 12 coins. Donald has 9 coins. How many more coins does Eileen have?

_____

Multiply and Divide with 8 and 7

Study Plan

---

1. Complete this function table.

Insects i	i	1		5	7		10
Legs $6 \times i$	l		24			54	

2. On this grid, dark segments have been drawn separating groups of 7, and the 7s count-bys have been circled. Describe two patterns you see.

1	11	21	31	41	51	61
2	12	22	32	42	52	62
3	13	23	33	43	53	63
4	14	24	34	44	54	64
5	15	25	35	45	55	65
6	16	26	36	46	56	66
7	17	27	37	47	57	67
8	18	28	38	48	58	68
9	19	29	39	49	59	69
10	20	30	40	50	60	70

_____

_____

_____

Find the unknown number in each Factor Triangle.

3.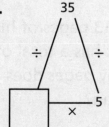

4.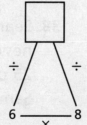

5.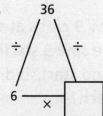

Remembering

Solve each multiplication and division problem.

1. $2 \cdot 7 =$ ___   **2.** $6 * 8 =$ ___   **3.** $10 \cdot 4 =$ ___   **4.** $8 * 8 =$ ___

5. $1 \times 10 =$ ___   **6.** $0 \times 9 =$ ___   **7.** $5 \times 3 =$ ___   **8.** $7 \times 9 =$ ___

9. $7 \cdot 8 =$ ___   **10.** $7 \times 1 =$ ___   **11.** $4 \cdot 8 =$ ___   **12.** $9 * 5 =$ ___

13. $9 \times 2 =$ ___   **14.** $7 * 7 =$ ___   **15.** $0 \cdot 2 =$ ___   **16.** $10 \times 1 =$ ___

17. $6\overline{)30}$ **18.** $72 \div 9 =$ ___   **19.** $30 / 3 =$ ___   **20.** $24 / 3 =$ ___

21. $18 / 6 =$ ___   **22.** $6\overline{)42}$ **23.** $6 \div 6 =$ ___   **24.** $32 / 8 =$ ___

25. $60 \div 6 =$ ___   **26.** $40 \div 5 =$ ___   **27.** $10\overline{)50}$ **28.** $81 \div 9 =$ ___

29. $36 / 6 =$ ___   **30.** $7\overline{)70}$ **31.** $21 \div 7 =$ ___   **32.** $36 / 9 =$ ___

33. $56 / 7 =$ ___   **34.** $4\overline{)40}$ **35.** $7 \div 1 =$ ___   **36.** $49 / 7 =$ ___

Solve each problem.

37. Sam saw 9 crabs at the beach. Then he saw 9 starfish. How many crabs and starfish did Sam see at the beach?

_____

38. Sean read the first 13 pages of his new book. His book has a total of 25 pages. How many pages does Sam have left to read?

_____

Homework

Name _____ **Date** _____

▶ Target Practice A

×	1	2	3	5	4	8	6	9	10	7
4	4	8	12	20	16	32	24	36	40	28
1	1	2	3	5	4	8	6	9	10	7
5	5	10	15	25	20	40	30	45	50	35
2	2	4	6	10	8	16	12	18	20	14
3	3	6	9	15	12	24	18	27	30	21
10	10	20	30	50	40	80	60	90	100	70
6	6	12	18	30	24	48	36	54	60	42
9	9	18	27	45	36	72	54	81	90	63
8	8	16	24	40	32	64	48	72	80	56
7	7	14	21	35	28	56	42	63	70	49

×	4	6	7	8
1	4	6	7	8
2	8	12	14	16
3	12	18	21	24
4	16	24	28	32
5	20	30	35	40
6	24	36	42	48
7	28	42	49	56
8	32	48	56	64
9	36	54	63	72
10	40	60	70	80

×	9	4	8	7	6	7	9	6	8	4
6	54	24	48	42	36	42	54	36	48	24
7	63	28	56	49	42	49	63	42	56	28
4	36	16	32	28	24	28	36	24	32	16
9	81	36	72	63	54	63	81	54	72	36
8	72	32	64	56	48	56	72	48	64	32
6	54	24	48	42	36	42	54	36	48	24
9	81	36	72	63	54	63	81	54	72	36
8	72	32	64	56	48	56	72	48	64	32
7	63	28	56	49	42	49	63	42	56	28
4	36	16	32	28	24	28	36	24	32	16

×	4	6	7	8
3	12	18	21	24
2	8	12	14	16
5	20	30	35	40
1	4	6	7	8
4	16	24	28	32
8	32	48	56	64
10	40	60	70	80
7	28	42	49	56
6	24	36	42	48
9	36	54	63	72

Name _____ Date _____

▶ Target Practice B

×	2	6	8	5	10	9	4	7	3	1
7	14	42	56	35	70	63	28	49	21	7
8	16	48	64	40	80	72	32	56	24	8
4	8	24	32	20	40	36	16	28	12	4
9	18	54	72	45	90	81	36	63	27	9
6	12	36	48	30	60	54	24	42	18	6
4	8	24	32	20	40	36	16	28	12	4
6	12	36	48	30	60	54	24	42	18	6
9	18	54	72	45	90	81	36	63	27	9
7	14	42	56	35	70	63	28	49	21	7
8	16	48	64	40	80	72	32	56	24	8

×	6	9	8	7	4
7	42	63	56	49	28
8	48	72	64	56	32
4	24	36	32	28	16
3	18	27	24	21	12
6	36	54	48	42	24
10	60	90	80	70	40
5	30	45	40	35	20
1	6	9	8	7	4
9	54	81	72	63	36
2	12	18	16	14	8

×	7	4	9	6	8	7	9	4	8	6
4	28	16	36	24	32	28	36	16	32	24
7	49	28	63	42	56	49	63	28	56	42
6	42	24	54	36	48	42	54	24	48	36
9	63	36	81	54	72	63	81	36	72	54
8	56	32	72	48	64	56	72	32	64	48
9	63	36	81	54	72	63	81	36	72	54
6	42	24	54	36	48	42	54	24	48	36
8	56	32	72	48	64	56	72	32	64	48
7	49	28	63	42	56	49	63	28	56	42
4	28	16	36	24	32	28	36	16	32	24

×	6	7	8	4	9
7	42	49	56	28	63
8	48	56	64	32	72
4	24	28	32	16	36
9	54	63	72	36	81
6	36	42	48	24	54
8	48	56	64	32	72
4	24	28	32	16	36
9	54	63	72	36	81
7	42	49	56	28	63
6	36	42	48	24	54

6×2

$6 \cdot 3$

$6 * 4$

6×5

Hint:
What is 2×6?
Copyright © Houghton Mifflin Company

Hint:
What is $3 \cdot 6$?
Copyright © Houghton Mifflin Company

Hint:
What is $4 * 6$?
Copyright © Houghton Mifflin Company

Hint:
What is 5×6?
Copyright © Houghton Mifflin Company

6×6

$6 \cdot 7$

$6 * 8$

6×9

Copyright © Houghton Mifflin Company

Hint:
What is $7 \cdot 6$?
Copyright © Houghton Mifflin Company

Hint:
What is $8 * 6$?
Copyright © Houghton Mifflin Company

Hint:
What is 9×6?
Copyright © Houghton Mifflin Company

7×2

$7 \cdot 3$

$7 * 4$

7×5

Hint:
What is 2×7?
Copyright © Houghton Mifflin Company

Hint:
What is $3 \cdot 7$?
Copyright © Houghton Mifflin Company

Hint:
What is $4 * 7$?
Copyright © Houghton Mifflin Company

Hint:
What is 5×7?
Copyright © Houghton Mifflin Company

7×6

$7 \cdot 7$

$7 * 8$

7×9

Hint:
What is 6×7?
Copyright © Houghton Mifflin Company

Copyright © Houghton Mifflin Company

Hint:
What is $8 * 7$?
Copyright © Houghton Mifflin Company

Hint:
What is 9×7?
Copyright © Houghton Mifflin Company

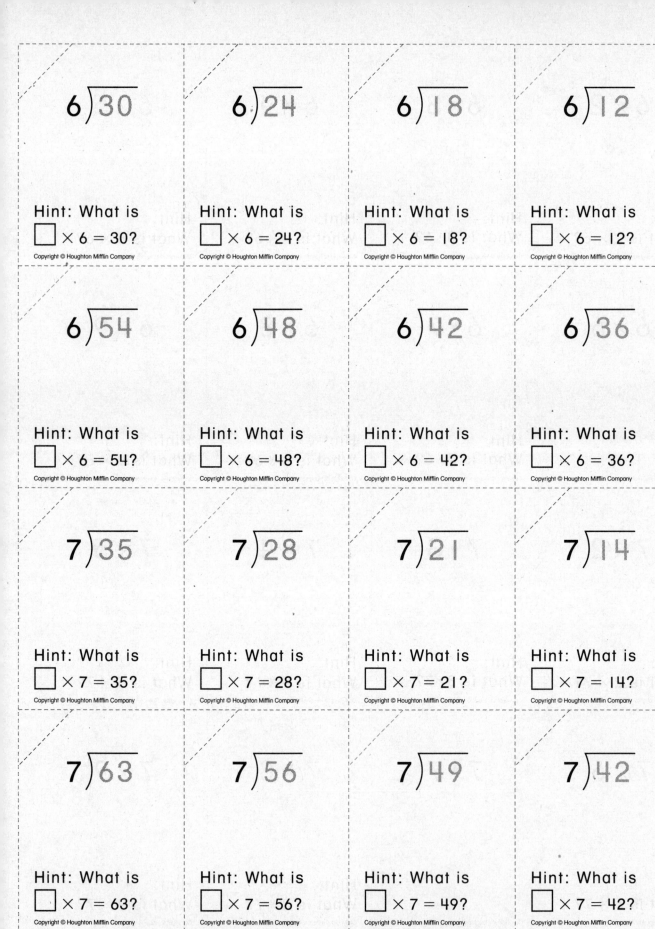

$6\overline{)30}$

Hint: What is
☐ × 6 = 30?

$6\overline{)24}$

Hint: What is
☐ × 6 = 24?

$6\overline{)18}$

Hint: What is
☐ × 6 = 18?

$6\overline{)12}$

Hint: What is
☐ × 6 = 12?

$6\overline{)54}$

Hint: What is
☐ × 6 = 54?

$6\overline{)48}$

Hint: What is
☐ × 6 = 48?

$6\overline{)42}$

Hint: What is
☐ × 6 = 42?

$6\overline{)36}$

Hint: What is
☐ × 6 = 36?

$7\overline{)35}$

Hint: What is
☐ × 7 = 35?

$7\overline{)28}$

Hint: What is
☐ × 7 = 28?

$7\overline{)21}$

Hint: What is
☐ × 7 = 21?

$7\overline{)14}$

Hint: What is
☐ × 7 = 14?

$7\overline{)63}$

Hint: What is
☐ × 7 = 63?

$7\overline{)56}$

Hint: What is
☐ × 7 = 56?

$7\overline{)49}$

Hint: What is
☐ × 7 = 49?

$7\overline{)42}$

Hint: What is
☐ × 7 = 42?

Product Cards: 6s, 7s, 8s

8×2

Hint:
What is 2×8?
Copyright © Houghton Mifflin Company

$8 \cdot 3$

Hint:
What is $3 \cdot 8$?
Copyright © Houghton Mifflin Company

$8 * 4$

Hint:
What is $4 * 8$?
Copyright © Houghton Mifflin Company

8×5

Hint:
What is 5×8?
Copyright © Houghton Mifflin Company

8×6

Hint:
What is 6×8?
Copyright © Houghton Mifflin Company

$8 \cdot 7$

Hint:
What is $7 \cdot 8$?
Copyright © Houghton Mifflin Company

$8 * 8$

Copyright © Houghton Mifflin Company

8×9

Hint:
What is 9×8?
Copyright © Houghton Mifflin Company

$\times$

$\cdot$

$*$

$\times$

$\times$

$\cdot$

$*$

$\times$

You can write any numbers on the last 8 cards. Use them to practice difficult problems or if you lose a card.

$8)\overline{40}$ $8)\overline{32}$ $8)\overline{24}$ $8)\overline{16}$

Hint: What is
$\square \times 8 = 40$?

Hint: What is
$\square \times 8 = 32$?

Hint: What is
$\square \times 8 = 24$?

Hint: What is
$\square \times 8 = 16$?

$8)\overline{72}$ $8)\overline{64}$ $8)\overline{56}$ $8)\overline{48}$

Hint: What is
$\square \times 8 = 72$?

Hint: What is
$\square \times 8 = 64$?

Hint: What is
$\square \times 8 = 56$?

Hint: What is
$\square \times 8 = 48$?

You can write any numbers on the last 8 cards. Use them to practice difficult problems or if you lose a card.

Product Cards: 6s, 7s, 8s

Name _____ **Date** _____

Homework

Study Plan

This pictograph shows the number of each type of muffin baked for the bake sale. Use the graph to solve problems 1–3.

1. How many chocolate chip muffins were baked?

_____

2. How many blueberry and cranberry muffins were baked altogether?

_____

3. How many more lemon muffins were baked than blueberry muffins?

_____

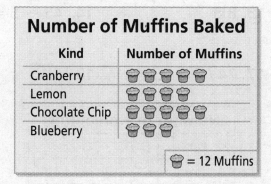

Number of Muffins Baked

Kind	Number of Muffins
Cranberry	
Lemon	
Chocolate Chip	
Blueberry	

= 12 Muffins

4. On a separate sheet of paper, describe a strategy for finding 6×12.

Solve each problem.

5. Bethany arranged some blocks in a square array. The array had 7 rows. How many blocks did she use in all?

_____

6. There are 11 students in Jennifer's math class. Each student needs 7 counters. How many counters are needed altogether?

_____

7. Fiona packed 48 eggs into cartons that hold one dozen eggs each. How many cartons did she use?
Hint: 1 dozen eggs = 12 eggs.

_____

8. Carl reserved 3 rows of seats, with 12 seats in each row. How many seats did Carl reserve?

_____

Remembering

Solve each multiplication and division problem.

1. 4 • 9 = ___　　　　**2.** 5 * 10 = ___　　　　**3.** 7 • 1 = ___　　　　**4.** 3 * 8 = ___

5. 10 × 2 = ___　　　**6.** 5 × 5 = ___　　　**7.** 1 × 9 = ___　　　**8.** 3 × 6 = ___

9. 4 • 7 = ___　　　**10.** 5 * 8 = ___　　　**11.** 8 • 2 = ___　　　**12.** 4 * 10 = ___

13. 8)8̄　　　　　　**14.** 45 ÷ 5 = ___　　**15.** 32 / 4 = ___　　**16.** 30 / 10 = ___

17. 24 / 4 = ___　　**18.** 5)15̄　　　　　　**19.** 12 ÷ 2 = ___　　**20.** 40 / 4 = ___

Number of Home Runs	
Pat	⚾ ⚾ ⚾
Juan	⚾ ⊟
Miguel	⚾ ⚾
Alan	⚾ ⚾ ⊟
	⚾ = 6 home runs

Use the pictograph for problems 21–25.

21. How many total home runs are shown? _____

22. How many more home runs does Pat have than Juan? _____

23. How many home runs do Miguel and Alan have altogether? _____

24. List the boys' names in order from greatest to least number of home runs.

_____

25. How many more home runs would Juan need in order to tie with Alan? _____

　　　　　　　　　　　　　　　Square Numbers, 11s, and 12s

$3\overline{)0}$	$9\overline{)10}$	$4\overline{)5}$	$9\overline{)1}$	$5\overline{)2}$	$2\overline{)5}$
$10\overline{)10}$	$3\overline{)2}$	$2\overline{)3}$	$9\overline{)7}$	$5\overline{)5}$	$4\overline{)2}$
$2\overline{)1}$	$5\overline{)3}$	$9\overline{)4}$	$10\overline{)0}$	$1\overline{)5}$	$5\overline{)10}$
$10\overline{)3}$	$9\overline{)5}$	$2\overline{)2}$	$4\overline{)4}$	$10\overline{)2}$	$3\overline{)9}$
$2\overline{)0}$	$9\overline{)2}$	$9\overline{)9}$	$1\overline{)9}$	$5\overline{)4}$	$10\overline{)9}$
$8\overline{)2}$	$1\overline{)10}$	$1\overline{)4}$	$4\overline{)10}$	$3\overline{)5}$	$2\overline{)10}$
$1\overline{)5}$	$1\overline{)1}$	$10\overline{)1}$	$5\overline{)1}$	$9\overline{)3}$	$4\overline{)1}$
$7\overline{)9}$	$1\overline{)2}$	$3\overline{)1}$	$4\overline{)9}$	$3\overline{)4}$	$9\overline{)0}$
$10\overline{)5}$	$1\overline{)3}$	$2\overline{)9}$	$2\overline{)4}$	$3\overline{)3}$	$3\overline{)10}$
$4\overline{)3}$	$10\overline{)4}$	$4\overline{)7}$	$5\overline{)7}$	$7\overline{)6}$	$5\overline{)9}$

$3\overline{)9}$	$1\overline{)10}$	$5\overline{)9}$	$4\overline{)1}$	$2\overline{)9}$	$10\overline{)10}$
$4\overline{)5}$	$9\overline{)4}$	$1\overline{)2}$	$3\overline{)1}$	$9\overline{)2}$	$4\overline{)10}$
$3\overline{)3}$	$10\overline{)9}$	$2\overline{)2}$	$4\overline{)4}$	$2\overline{)3}$	$3\overline{)4}$
$1\overline{)3}$	$10\overline{)5}$	$9\overline{)5}$	$10\overline{)3}$	$4\overline{)7}$	$4\overline{)3}$
$9\overline{)7}$	$5\overline{)2}$	$2\overline{)5}$	$5\overline{)5}$	$9\overline{)3}$	$9\overline{)0}$
$2\overline{)4}$	$10\overline{)4}$	$7\overline{)6}$	$5\overline{)7}$	$1\overline{)4}$	$3\overline{)5}$
$4\overline{)2}$	$9\overline{)1}$	$2\overline{)10}$	$7\overline{)7}$	$9\overline{)10}$	$2\overline{)1}$
$10\overline{)0}$	$1\overline{)5}$	$5\overline{)3}$	$10\overline{)2}$	$5\overline{)4}$	$3\overline{)0}$
$1\overline{)9}$	$3\overline{)2}$	$1\overline{)5}$	$2\overline{)0}$	$4\overline{)9}$	$5\overline{)1}$
$1\overline{)1}$	$10\overline{)1}$	$7\overline{)9}$	$8\overline{)2}$	$3\overline{)10}$	$9\overline{)9}$

Home Write-On Sheet 2B

$$
\begin{array}{cccccc}
\overset{0}{3\overline{)0}} & \overset{10}{9\overline{)90}} & \overset{5}{4\overline{)20}} & \overset{1}{9\overline{)9}} & \overset{2}{5\overline{)10}} & \overset{5}{2\overline{)10}} \\[2em]
\overset{10}{10\overline{)100}} & \overset{2}{3\overline{)6}} & \overset{3}{2\overline{)6}} & \overset{7}{9\overline{)63}} & \overset{5}{5\overline{)25}} & \overset{2}{4\overline{)8}} \\[2em]
\overset{1}{2\overline{)2}} & \overset{3}{5\overline{)15}} & \overset{4}{9\overline{)36}} & \overset{0}{10\overline{)0}} & \overset{5}{1\overline{)5}} & \overset{10}{5\overline{)50}} \\[2em]
\overset{3}{10\overline{)30}} & \overset{5}{9\overline{)45}} & \overset{2}{2\overline{)4}} & \overset{4}{4\overline{)16}} & \overset{2}{10\overline{)20}} & \overset{9}{3\overline{)27}} \\[2em]
\overset{0}{2\overline{)0}} & \overset{2}{9\overline{)18}} & \overset{9}{9\overline{)81}} & \overset{9}{1\overline{)9}} & \overset{4}{5\overline{)20}} & \overset{9}{10\overline{)90}} \\[2em]
\overset{2}{8\overline{)16}} & \overset{10}{1\overline{)10}} & \overset{4}{1\overline{)4}} & \overset{10}{4\overline{)40}} & \overset{5}{3\overline{)15}} & \overset{10}{2\overline{)20}} \\[2em]
\overset{5}{1\overline{)5}} & \overset{1}{1\overline{)1}} & \overset{1}{10\overline{)10}} & \overset{1}{5\overline{)5}} & \overset{3}{9\overline{)27}} & \overset{1}{4\overline{)4}} \\[2em]
\overset{9}{7\overline{)63}} & \overset{2}{1\overline{)2}} & \overset{1}{3\overline{)3}} & \overset{9}{4\overline{)36}} & \overset{4}{3\overline{)12}} & \overset{0}{9\overline{)0}} \\[2em]
\overset{5}{10\overline{)50}} & \overset{3}{1\overline{)3}} & \overset{9}{2\overline{)18}} & \overset{4}{2\overline{)8}} & \overset{3}{3\overline{)9}} & \overset{10}{3\overline{)30}} \\[2em]
\overset{3}{4\overline{)12}} & \overset{4}{10\overline{)40}} & \overset{7}{4\overline{)28}} & \overset{7}{5\overline{)35}} & \overset{6}{7\overline{)42}} & \overset{9}{5\overline{)45}}
\end{array}
$$

9 $3\overline{)27}$	10 $1\overline{)10}$	9 $5\overline{)45}$	1 $4\overline{)4}$	9 $2\overline{)18}$	10 $10\overline{)100}$
5 $4\overline{)20}$	4 $9\overline{)36}$	2 $1\overline{)2}$	1 $3\overline{)3}$	2 $9\overline{)18}$	10 $4\overline{)40}$
3 $3\overline{)9}$	9 $10\overline{)90}$	2 $2\overline{)4}$	4 $4\overline{)16}$	3 $2\overline{)6}$	4 $3\overline{)12}$
3 $1\overline{)3}$	5 $10\overline{)50}$	5 $9\overline{)45}$	3 $10\overline{)30}$	7 $4\overline{)28}$	3 $4\overline{)12}$
7 $9\overline{)63}$	2 $5\overline{)10}$	5 $2\overline{)10}$	5 $5\overline{)25}$	3 $9\overline{)27}$	0 $9\overline{)0}$
4 $2\overline{)8}$	4 $10\overline{)40}$	6 $7\overline{)42}$	7 $5\overline{)35}$	4 $1\overline{)4}$	5 $3\overline{)15}$
2 $4\overline{)8}$	1 $9\overline{)9}$	10 $2\overline{)20}$	7 $7\overline{)49}$	10 $9\overline{)90}$	1 $2\overline{)2}$
0 $10\overline{)0}$	5 $1\overline{)5}$	3 $5\overline{)15}$	2 $10\overline{)20}$	4 $5\overline{)20}$	0 $3\overline{)0}$
9 $1\overline{)9}$	2 $3\overline{)6}$	5 $1\overline{)5}$	0 $2\overline{)0}$	9 $4\overline{)36}$	1 $5\overline{)5}$
1 $1\overline{)1}$	1 $10\overline{)10}$	9 $7\overline{)63}$	2 $8\overline{)16}$	10 $3\overline{)30}$	9 $9\overline{)81}$

Homework

Study Plan

Write your answers for problems 1 and 2 on a separate sheet of paper.

1. Does $(a - b) - c = a - (b - c)$ for all numbers a, b, and c? Explain and show an example.

2. Does $a \cdot (b - c) = a \cdot b - a \cdot c$ for all numbers a, b, and c? Explain and show an example.

Name the property used in each equation.

3. $1 \cdot 37 = 37$

_____

_____

4. $4 \times 25 = 25 \times 4$

_____

_____

5. $2 \cdot (60 + 3) = (2 \cdot 60) + (2 \cdot 3)$

_____

_____

6. $(2 \times 3) \times 6 = 2 \times (3 \times 6)$

_____

_____

Use a property to find the value of n.

7. $54 \times 6 = 6 \times n$

_____

8. $3 \times (10 + 6) = (3 \times 10) + (3 \times n)$

_____

9. $16 \times n = 16$

_____

10. $(5 \times 1) \times 8 = 5 \times (1 \times n)$

_____

11. $(n \times 2) \times 10 = 5 \times (2 \times 10)$

_____

12. $3 \times n = 20 \times 3$

_____

Remembering

Solve each multiplication and division problem.

1. $5 \cdot 6 =$ ___

2. $2 * 1 =$ ___

3. $7 \cdot 4 =$ ___

4. $6 * 8 =$ ___

5. $5 \times 5 =$ ___

6. $10 \times 3 =$ ___

7. $1 \times 3 =$ ___

8. $4 \times 9 =$ ___

9. $3 \cdot 8 =$ ___

10. $2 \times 6 =$ ___

11. $6 \cdot 10 =$ ___

12. $9 * 2 =$ ___

13. $8 \times 5 =$ ___

14. $4 * 7 =$ ___

15. $10 \cdot 2 =$ ___

16. $6 \times 1 =$ ___

17. $4\overline{)32}$

18. $54 \div 9 =$ ___

19. $40 / 4 =$ ___

20. $15 / 3 =$ ___

21. $36 / 6 =$ ___

22. $3\overline{)21}$

23. $42 \div 6 =$ ___

24. $80 / 8 =$ ___

25. $24 \div 4 =$ ___

26. $5 \div 5 =$ ___

27. $1\overline{)5}$

28. $45 \div 9 =$ ___

29. $54 / 6 =$ ___

30. $3\overline{)12}$

31. $14 \div 2 =$ ___

32. $50 / 10 =$ ___

33. $30 / 5 =$ ___

34. $2\overline{)12}$

35. $3 \div 1 =$ ___

36. $18 / 6 =$ ___

Solve each problem.

37. Gerald picked 7 tulips and 14 daffodils and put them in a vase. How many flowers does he have in his vase?

_____

38. Sally lives 8 blocks from school. Maria lives 11 blocks from school. How many more blocks does Maria live from the school?

_____

Properties of Multiplication

Homework

Study Plan

Complete this function table.

1.

Dozens of Eggs d	d	1		5	7		11
Number of Eggs $12 \cdot d$	n		36			108	

Fill in the missing number in each Fast Array.

2.

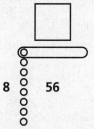

8   56

3.

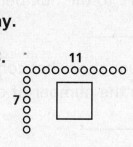

11

7

Solve each problem.

4. Marisa's age is 4 times Sam's age. Marisa is 20 years old. How old is Sam?

_____

5. Raul and Rosa were playing basketball. Raul made 10 baskets. Rosa made half as many as Raul. How many baskets did Rosa make?

_____

6. Jeff sold 12 cars on Friday. He sold 3 times as many cars on Saturday. How many cars did Jeff sell on Saturday?

_____

7. Danielle received $32 for her birthday. Three years ago, she received $\frac{1}{4}$ as much. How much did Danielle receive three years ago?

_____

Remembering

Use the shapes to answer exercises 1–5.

1. How many circles? How many rectangles? Use multiplication to find the answers.

   _____

2. Because 6 × _____ = 12, there are _____ times as many circles as rectangles.

3. Because 12 ÷ _____ = 6, there are _____ as many rectangles as circles.

4. Write a multiplication equation that compares the number of circles c to the number of rectangles r.

   _____

5. Write a division equation that compares the number of rectangles r to the number of circles c.

   _____

Multiply or divide.

6. $1 \times 7 =$ __   7. $42 \div 6 =$ __   8. $11 \times 3 =$ __   9. $24 \div 8 =$ __

10. $99 \div 9 =$ __   11. $4 \times 12 =$ __   12. $8 \times 6 =$ __   13. $12 \div 3 =$ __

14. $0 \times 7 =$ __   15. $9 \div 1 =$ __   16. $40 \div 8 =$ __   17. $12 \times 2 =$ __

18. $40 \div 10 =$ __   19. $2 \times 7 =$ __   20. $3 \times 9 =$ __   21. $36 \div 6 =$ __

22. $1 \times 1 =$ __   23. $49 \div 7 =$ __   24. $10 \times 9 =$ __   25. $0 \div 5 =$ __

26. $35 \div 5 =$ __   27. $2 \times 10 =$ __   28. $6 \times 3 =$ __   29. $28 \div 4 =$ __

Name _____ **Date** _____

Homework

Study Plan

Use the table to solve problems 1–4.

1. What is the depth of Crater Lake?

_____

2. How many lakes in the table are
in the United States?

_____

3. What is the deepest lake in the table?

_____

4. What is the difference in depth
between Malawi Lake and
Tahoe Lake?

_____

Lake	Location	Depth (feet)
Baikal	Russia	5,371
Crater	United States	1,932
Hornindals	Norway	1,686
Malawi	Malawi and Mozambique	2,316
Tahoe	United States	1,657

5. Ask four friends or family members their age and
favorite color. Then complete the table.

Name	Age	Favorite Color

6. On a separate sheet of paper, write two questions that
can be answered using your table.

Remembering

Solve each multiplication and division problem.

1. $7 \cdot 6 =$ __   2. $2 * 10 =$ __   3. $3 \cdot 9 =$ __   4. $7 * 8 =$ __

5. $9 \times 6 =$ __   6. $1 \times 8 =$ __   7. $8 * 5 =$ __   8. $2 \times 7 =$ __

9. $10 \cdot 7 =$ __   10. $7 * 7 =$ __   11. $5 \cdot 6 =$ __   12. $4 * 6 =$ __

13. $5\overline{)50}$ 14. $8 \div 8 =$ __   15. $64 / 8 =$ __   16. $63 / 7 =$ __

17. $24 / 8 =$ __   18. $1\overline{)9}$ 19. $25 \div 5 =$ __   20. $80 / 10 =$ __

21. $32 \div 4 =$ __   22. $12 \div 6 =$ __   23. $6\overline{)30}$ 24. $48 \div 8 =$ __

25. Write eight equations based on this factor triangle.

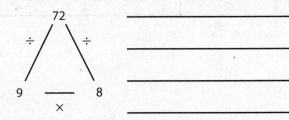

_____   _____

_____   _____

_____   _____

_____   _____

Simplify each expression.

26. $4 \cdot (8 - 2)$ _____   27. $4 \cdot 8 - 2$ _____

Solve each problem.

28. Allison practiced the piano for 30 minutes. Her brother Sean practiced for 20 minutes. How many more minutes did Allison practice?

_____

29. A farmer had 18 boxes of strawberries to sell. By the afternoon, the farmer sold 6 boxes. How many boxes does the farmer have left to sell?

_____

Solve Word Problems with Tables

Homework

Study Plan

Write a situation and a solution equation, using a letter to represent the unknown. Solve your equations. Make a math drawing, if you wish.

1. A small truck can hold 35 boxes of toys. Five boxes fit across the width of the truck. How many boxes fit along the length of the truck?

Situation Equation: _____

Solution Equation: _____

2. People in a marching band stand in 8 equal rows. There are 56 people in the band. How many people are in each row?

Situation Equation: _____

Solution Equation: _____

3. Mr. Rodriguez is putting 63 post cards from Venezuela on a bulletin board. He is putting them in equal rows of 7 post cards. How many rows does he have?

Situation Equation: _____

Solution Equation: _____

4. Crystal's ballet class has 36 dancers who are dancing in a recital. For the first dance, they will enter the stage in groups of 4 dancers. How many groups will there be?

Situation Equation: _____

Solution Equation: _____

Remembering

Solve each multiplication and division problem.

1. $12 \cdot 4 =$ ___ **2.** $9 * 5 =$ ___ **3.** $8 \times 9 =$ ___ **4.** $11 * 5 =$ ___

5. $14 \div 2 =$ ___ **6.** $60 \div 10 =$ ___ **7.** $0 \cdot 12 =$ ___ **8.** $48 \div 6 =$ ___

Use a property to find the value of n.

9. $6 \times 11 = 11 \times n$

_____

10. $65 \times n = 0$

_____

11. $3 \times (2 \times n) = (3 \times 2) \times 5$

_____

12. $7 \times (2 + n) = (7 \times 2) + (7 \times 1)$

_____

13. $(4 \times 6) \times 10 = 4 \times (n \times 10)$

_____

14. $42 \times n = 42$

_____

Simplify each expression.

15. $(6 + 2) \times 4 =$ _____

16. $6 + 2 \times 4 =$ _____

17. $5 \cdot (11 - 6) =$ _____

18. $5 \cdot 11 - 6 =$ _____

Write a situation and a solution equation, using a letter to represent the unknown. Solve your equations.

19. Mrs. O'Hara has a collection of 45 thimbles. She displays them in a case that has 5 equal rows. How many thimbles are in each row?

Situation Equation: _____

Solution Equation: _____

20. There are 3 times as many students in an art club as there are in a science club. If there are 24 students in the art club, how many students are in the science club?

Situation Equation: _____

Solution Equation: _____

Name _____ **Date** _____

Homework

Use the shapes to answer exercises 1–5.

1. How many squares? How many triangles? Use multiplication to find the answers.

_____

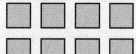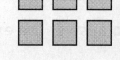

2. Because 4 × _____ = 12, there are _____ times as many squares as triangles.

3. Because 12 ÷ _____ = 4, there are _____ as many triangles as squares.

4. Write a multiplication equation that compares the number of squares s to the number of triangles t. _____

5. Write a division equation that compares the number of triangles t to the number of squares s. _____

Solve each problem.

6. Elena's age is 6 times Victor's age. Elena is 12 years old. How many years old is Victor?

_____

7. Megan walked 6 kilometers. This distance is 6 times as many kilometers as Marco walked. What distance did Marco walk?

_____

Remembering

Multiply or divide.

1. $36 \div 6 =$ ___

2. $5 \times 8 =$ ___

3. $7 \times 9 =$ ___

4. $56 \div 8 =$ ___

5. $5 \times 7 =$ ___

6. $72 \div 9 =$ ___

7. $42 \div 7 =$ ___

8. $5 \times 6 =$ ___

Simplify each expression.

9. $8 - (4 \cdot 2) =$ _____

10. $8 - 4 \cdot 2 =$ _____

11. $10 \cdot (5 + 2) =$ _____

12. $10 \cdot 5 + 2 =$ _____

Use the pictograph to answer the exercises.

Number of Points Scored	
Team 1	⚽ ⚽ ⚽
Team 2	⚽ ⚽ ⚽ ⚽
Team 3	⚽ ⚽ ⚽ ⚽ ⚽ ⚽
Team 4	⚽ ⚽

⚽ = 8 points

13. What two combined team scores equal 80 points?

_____

14. What team scored the most points? How many?

_____

15. How many more points did Team 2 score than Team 4?

_____

16. Write the team names in order of their scores, from greatest to least.

_____

_____

17. How many more points would Team 4 have needed to tie with Team 3?

_____

18. Write a number sentence comparing Team 2's points (*t*) and Team 4's points (*f*).

_____

Multiplication Comparisons

Homework

Name _____ **Date** _____

Study Plan

Use the graph to answer exercises 1–4.

1. How tall is a polar bear? _____

2. Which animal is the tallest? _____
How tall is it? _____

3. Which animal is the shortest? _____
How tall is it? _____

4. What is the difference in height
between the tallest and the shortest
animals? _____

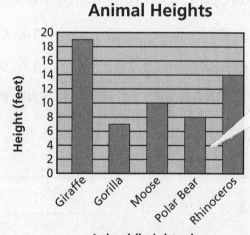

Animal Heights

Height (feet)

Giraffe Gorilla Moose Polar Bear Rhinoceros

Animal (height when
animal is on all fours)

**Use the information below to make a
horizontal bar graph.**

5.   **Number of Gold Medals Won at the 2002 Winter Olympics**

Country	China	Germany	Italy	United States
Gold Medals	2	12	4	10

Remembering

Complete each multiplication and division equation.

1. $16 = 8 \times$ _____

2. $25 =$ _____ $\times 5$

3. _____ $= 4 \times 8$

4. $54 = 6 \times$ _____

5. $4 =$ _____ $\times 2$

6. _____ $= 2 \times 6$

7. $3 = 6 \div$ _____

8. $6 =$ _____ $\div 4$

9. _____ $= 12 \div 4$

10. $9 = 45 \div$ _____

11. $9 =$ _____ $\div 3$

12. _____ $= 80 \div 8$

Solve each division as quickly as you can. Then circle any that you need to practice more.

13. $24 \div 6 =$ _____

14. $64 \div 8 =$ _____

15. $32 \div 8 =$ _____

16. $63 / 7 =$ _____

17. $36 / 6 =$ _____

18. $54 / 6 =$ _____

19. $8\overline{)40} =$ _____

20. $8\overline{)56} =$ _____

21. $7\overline{)28} =$ _____

Simplify each expression.

22. $(6 * 6) \div 3 =$ _____

23. $6 * (6 \div 3) =$ _____

24. $8 \times (5 + 4) =$ _____

25. $8 \times 5 + 4 =$ _____

Solve each problem.

26. Angela sold 7 cakes on Monday. She sold 14 cakes on Wednesday. How many cakes did she sell altogether?

_____

27. Each week, Tanya bicycles 9 miles. Damon bicycles 11 miles. How many more miles does Damon bicycle?

_____

Write a situation and a solution equation, using a letter to represent the unknown. Solve your equations.

28. Mina is in a class of 18 students. Six students sit in each row. How many rows are there?

Situation Equation:

_____

Solution Equation:

_____

29. Min Ho's collection of 32 marbles is 4 times the size of Ryan's collection. How many marbles does Ryan have?

Situation Equation:

_____

Solution Equation:

_____

Name _____   **Date** _____

Homework

Study Plan

Solve each problem.

1. $5 \times 7 + 9 =$

_____

2. $9 \times (1 + 3) =$

_____

3. $7 - 2 \times 2 =$

_____

4. $(7 \times 2) + (4 \times 9) =$

_____

5. $(6 - 2) \times 8 =$

_____

6. $2 \times 6 - 4 =$

_____

7. $(7 - 2) \times (3 + 2) =$

_____

8. $8 \times (12 - 7) =$

_____

9. Whitney and Georgia are at the snack bar. They are buying food for their family. Sandwiches cost $4 each. Salads cost $2 each. How much will it cost them to buy 5 sandwiches and 7 salads?

_____

10. Lisa put tulips and roses into vases. Each vase has 12 flowers. The red vase has 7 tulips. The blue vase has twice as many roses as the red vase. How many roses are in the blue vase?

_____

11. Pam has 9 bags of apples. Each bag contains 6 apples. There are 3 bags of red apples and 1 bag of green apples. The rest of the bags contain yellow apples. How many more yellow apples are there than red apples?

_____

12. Clay works on a farm. He packaged eggs into containers that hold 1 dozen eggs each. He filled 4 containers with white eggs and 5 containers with brown eggs. How many eggs did Clay collect? Hint: one dozen eggs = 12 eggs

_____

Remembering

Solve each problem.

A teacher at Lakeside School surveyed the students about their pets. The bar graph shows all the pets in the families of all the students. Use the bar graph to complete exercises 1–3.

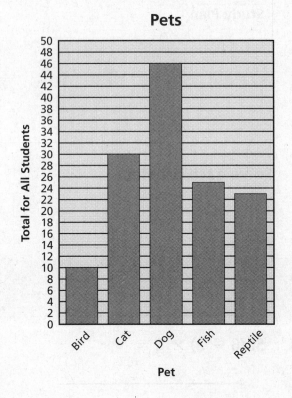

Pets

1. The number of _____ is $\frac{1}{2}$ the number of dogs.

2. The number of _____ is 3 times the number of birds.

3. The number of pets in all the families of all the students is _____

Multiply or divide.

4. $6 \times 5 =$ ___   **5.** $32 \div 4 =$ ___   **6.** $12 \times 3 =$ ___   **7.** $72 \div 8 =$ ___

8. $36 \div 9 =$ ___   **9.** $11 \times 8 =$ ___   **10.** $7 \times 6 =$ ___   **11.** $80 \div 8 =$ ___

12. $4 \times 6 =$ ___   **13.** $16 \div 4 =$ ___   **14.** $56 \div 8 =$ ___   **15.** $7 \times 0 =$ ___

16. $22 \div 2 =$ ___   **17.** $5 \times 5 =$ ___   **18.** $6 \times 2 =$ ___   **19.** $28 \div 7 =$ ___

20. $7 \times 1 =$ ___   **21.** $18 \div 9 =$ ___   **22.** $5 \times 3 =$ ___   **23.** $12 \div 4 =$ ___

Simplify each expression.

24. $5 \times 3 \times 2 =$ _____

25. $5 \times (3 \times 2) =$ _____

26. $5 + 3 \times 2 =$ _____

27. $(5 + 3) \times 2 =$ _____

Homework

Study Plan

_____

List the factor pairs for each number.

1. 35 _____

2. 17 _____

3. 28 _____

4. Make two different Factor Fireworks for 64.

5. Write an equation that shows 64 as a product of prime numbers.

   _____

6. Use your equation to help you find 64 ÷ 16.

   _____

7. Make two different Factor Fireworks for 84.

8. Write an equation that shows 84 as a product of prime factors. Then use your equation to help you find 84 ÷ 12 and 84 ÷ 21.

   _____

   _____

Name _____ **Date** _____

Remembering

Students in the fourth grade chose their favorite color from 5 choices. The bar graph shows the results.

Use the graph for exercises 1–3.

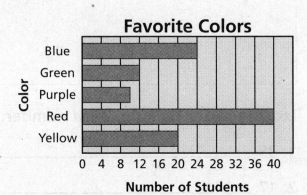

Favorite Colors

1. Which color did $\frac{1}{2}$ as many students choose as blue?

   _____

2. Which color did 4 times as many students choose as purple?

   _____

3. How many students were asked?

   _____

Multiply or divide.

4. $12 \times 5 =$ ___   5. $40 \div 4 =$ ___   6. $9 \times 6 =$ ___   7. $32 \div 8 =$ ___

8. $90 \div 10 =$ ___   9. $7 \times 2 =$ ___   10. $9 \times 3 =$ ___   11. $42 \div 6 =$ ___

12. $11 \times 6 =$ ___   13. $81 \div 9 =$ ___   14. $24 \div 8 =$ ___   15. $0 \times 12 =$ ___

16. $56 \div 7 =$ ___   17. $3 \times 12 =$ ___   18. $4 \times 7 =$ ___   19. $44 \div 4 =$ ___

20. $1 \times 9 =$ ___   21. $24 \div 6 =$ ___   22. $7 \times 9 =$ ___   23. $15 \div 3 =$ ___

24. $16 \div 4 =$ ___   25. $10 \times 0 =$ ___   26. $12 \times 4 =$ ___   27. $40 \div 8 =$ ___

Solve each problem. Write an equation, if you wish.

28. The Polk family hiked a 19-mile trail. The Ortíz family hiked a 26-mile trail. How much farther did the Ortíz family hike?

29. Melanie's stamp book has 40 equal spaces on each page for stamps. If there are 8 rows, how many stamps are in each row?

_____   _____

Factors and Prime Numbers

1. Connections

Roberto made a path that is 10 feet long. He decides to make the path 24 inches longer. Will the path be 12 feet or 12 inches long? Explain.

_____

_____

_____

2. Reasoning and Proof

Support or disprove the following statement with examples.

An even number times an odd number is an even number.

_____

_____

3. Communication

2	12
3	18
4	24
5	?
6	36

What number is missing from this table? Explain.

_____

_____

_____

4. Representation

Show the following data in a bar graph. Use grid paper.

Number of Dinners Served

Day of Week	Number of Dinners
Monday	52
Tuesday	46
Wednesday	58
Thursday	39

Remembering

Multiply or divide.

1. $4 \times 6 =$ _____

2. $42 \div 7 =$ _____

3. $9 \times 1 =$ _____

4. $18 \div 3 =$ _____

5. $5 \times 3 =$ _____

6. $25 \div 5 =$ _____

7. $64 \div 8 =$ _____

8. $8 \times 0 =$ _____

9. $8 \times 7 =$ _____

10. $9 \times 8 =$ _____

11. $12 \div 3 =$ _____

12. $21 \div 7 =$ _____

13. $60 \div 6 =$ _____

14. $11 \times 9 =$ _____

15. $45 \div 9 =$ _____

16. $10 \times 5 =$ _____

17. $55 \div 5 =$ _____

18. $7 \times 7 =$ _____

Simplify each expression.

19. $6 + 4 \times 3 =$ _____

20. $8 - 5 + 4 =$ _____

Solve each problem.

21. Lupe bought 19 books from one store and 7 books from another store. How many books did she buy all together?

_____

22. Jason had 17 stamps. He gave 9 stamps to a friend. How many stamps did he have left?

_____

23. Karen has 19 horse statues. Mio has 10 horse statues. How many fewer horse statues does Mio have?

_____

24. Chen scored 3 soccer goals on Monday and 2 soccer goals on Tuesday. How many soccer goals did he score in all?

_____

Use Mathematical Processes

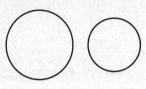

Name _____ Date _____

Homework

Tell whether each pair of figures looks congruent.

1.
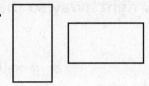

2.

3.
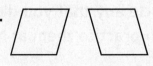

_____

4.
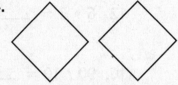

5.
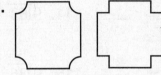

6.
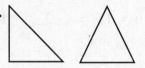

_____

Tell whether the dotted line is a line of symmetry.

7.
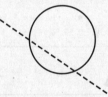

8.

9.
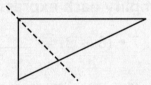

_____

How many lines of symmetry does each figure have?

10.

11.
 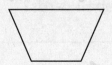

12.

_____

Circle the figures that appear to be similar.

13.

Remembering

Solve each multiplication or division as quickly as you can.
Circle any that you didn't know right away so that you
can practice them at home.

1. $3 \cdot 4 = $ ___   **2.** $5\overline{)30}$ 3. $4 \times 0 = $ ___   4. $9 \cdot 9 = $ ___

5. $15 / 5 = $ ___   6. $9 * 5 = $ ___   7. $28 / 4 = $ ___   8. $4 \cdot 1 = $ ___

9. $5 * 10 = $ ___   10. $3 \div 3 = $ ___   11. $9\overline{)63}$ 12. $6 \cdot 3 = $ ___

13. $0 / 10 = $ ___   14. $8 * 4 = $ ___   15. $9\overline{)36}$ 16. $90 / 10 = $ ___

17. $6 \cdot 9 = $ ___   18. $5 * 5 = $ ___   19. $20 \div 4 = $ ___   20. $3\overline{)21}$

Simplify each expression.

21. $7 \cdot (6 - 3) = $ _____   22. $7 \cdot 6 - 3 = $ _____

23. $(9 \times 7) - 5 = $ _____   24. $9 \times (7 - 5) = $ _____

Joe has one dozen baseball cards to share.
Answer each question.

Show your work.

25. If Joe gives 3 cards to Juan and 4 to Donya, how
    many cards will Joe still have?

    _____

26. If Joe gives away some of his cards and has 9 cards
    left, how many cards did he give away?

    _____

27. If Joe gives each of his friends 2 baseball cards,
    to how many friends can he give baseball cards?

    _____

Congruence and Symmetry

Name _____   **Date** _____

Homework

Vocabulary

square
isosceles
 trapezoid
trapezoid
rhombus
rectangle
parallelogram

Using the Vocabulary box to the right, write the name of the quadrilateral that best describes each figure. Use each word once. Describe how it is different from other quadrilaterals.

1.

_____

_____

_____

2.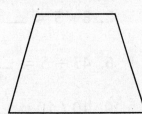

_____

_____

_____

3.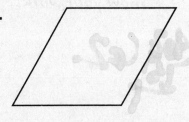

_____

_____

_____

4.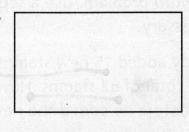

_____

_____

_____

5.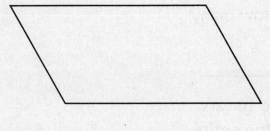

_____

_____

_____

6.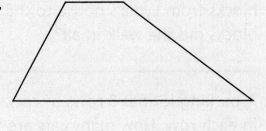

_____

_____

_____

Kinds of Quadrilaterals **77**

Remembering

Solve each multiplication or division as quickly as you can. Circle any that you didn't know right away so that you can practice them at home.

1. $9 \cdot 4 =$ _____   **2.** $8 * 5 =$ _____   **3.** $3\overline{)6}$ **4.** $3 \times 2 =$ _____

5. $80 / 10 =$ _____   **6.** $45 \div 5 =$ _____   **7.** $2 * 10 =$ _____   **8.** $0 \times 8 =$ _____

9. $4\overline{)32}$ **10.** $10 / 10 =$ _____   **11.** $8 \cdot 3 =$ _____   **12.** $7 * 10 =$ _____

13. $0 \div 9 =$ _____   **14.** $4\overline{)12}$ **15.** $3 \times 9 =$ _____   **16.** $16 / 2 =$ _____

Simplify each expression.

17. $(12 - 3) \times 2 =$ _____   **18.** $12 - (3 \times 2) =$ _____

Solve each word problem. Use a separate sheet of paper if necessary.

Show your work.

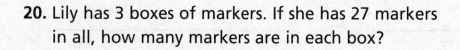

19. After Rudy added 15 new stamps to his collection, he had a total of 62 stamps. How many stamps did he have before he added the new ones?

_____

20. Lily has 3 boxes of markers. If she has 27 markers in all, how many markers are in each box?

_____

21. Bala walked 3 blocks to Lydia's house and 5 more blocks from Lydia's house to the library. How many blocks did she walk in all?

_____

22. A parking lot has 8 rows of cars. There are 10 cars in each row. How many cars are there in the entire parking lot?

_____

Kinds of Quadrilaterals

Homework

On a separate sheet of paper, sketch a rectangle for each exercise. Choose a measurement unit for each rectangle and find the area and perimeter. Show your work.

1. 5 by 6   **2.** 8 by 4   **3.** 7 by 5   **4.** 4 by 7

5. Challenge Using only whole numbers, make as many different rectangles as you can that have either the same area or the same perimeter as the rectangles in exercises 1–4.

Solve each word problem. Draw a picture if you need to.   *Show your work.*

6. Enzo is building a dog run that measures 10 feet by 9 feet. How many feet of fencing does he need to fence in the area?

_____

_____

7. A sheet of construction paper is 9 inches across and 11 inches high. How many 1-inch squares of paper can Dwayne cut out of one sheet of paper?

_____

_____

8. Mieko has a rug that is 6 feet long and 8 feet wide. Her room measures 9 feet each way. Will the rug fit in her room? How do you know?

_____

_____

_____

Name _____ **Date** _____

Remembering

Solve each multiplication or division as quickly as you can. Circle any that you didn't know right away so that you can practice them at home.

1. $2 \cdot 0 =$ ____   **2.** $3 \times 1 =$ ____   **3.** $9 * 5 =$ ____   **4.** $8 \cdot 10 =$ ____

5. $4 * 9 =$ ____   **6.** $2 \times 5 =$ ____   **7.** $24 / 3 =$ ____   **8.** $100 / 10 =$ ____

9. $36 \div 4 =$ ____   **10.** $0 / 3 =$ ____   **11.** $9\overline{)63}$ **12.** $15 / 5 =$ ____

13. $7 * 2 =$ ____   **14.** $18 \div 9 =$ ____   **15.** $9\overline{)54}$ **16.** $4 \cdot 5 =$ ____

Simplify each expression.

17. $2 \times (12 \div 4) =$ _____   **18.** $2 \times 12 \div 4 =$ _____

19. $(14 + 6) \times 5 =$ _____   **20.** $14 + 6 \times 5 =$ _____

Solve each word problem.   *Show your work.*

21. Polly and her father went fishing. Each of them caught 4 fish every day. They were away for a week. How many fish did they catch in all?

_____

22. There are 72 pages in a book. If you read 8 pages a day, how many days will it take you to finish the book?

_____

23. There are 10 seats in each row of the school auditorium and 10 rows of seats in each section. Can all 93 fourth-graders sit together in one section of the auditorium? How do you know?

_____

_____

Perimeter and Area of Rectangles

Name each figure and find its perimeter.

1.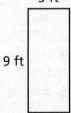
3 ft

9 ft

_____

_____

2.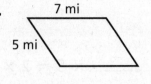
7 mi

5 mi

_____

_____

3.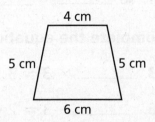
4 cm

5 cm   5 cm

6 cm

_____

_____

Name each quadrilateral and find its area.

4.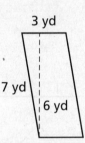
3 yd

7 yd

6 yd

_____

_____

5.
7 m

7 m

_____

_____

6.
6 in.

6 in.   5 in.

_____

_____

7. Write the formula for the perimeter and area of a rectangle and of a parallelogram.

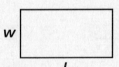
w   l

s   h
b

_____

_____

Solve the problems. Use a drawing to help you.

8. Aaron's yard is 9 meters long and 8 meters wide. He wants to plant sod grass in the entire yard. How many 1-meter × 1-meter squares of sod grass does he need?

_____

9. Aaron also wants to fence in the yard. How many meters of fencing would Aaron need to fence in the entire yard?

_____

Remembering

Write two different factor pairs for each number.

1. 18 _____ _____

2. 12 _____ _____

Complete the equation.

3. _____ × 3 = 3 × 8

4. _____ × 5 = 2 × 10

5. _____ × 9 = 3 × 3

6. _____ ÷ 3 = 2 ÷ 2

7. _____ ÷ 1 = 12 ÷ 4

8. _____ × 3 = 2 × 0

Name each figure.

9.

_____

10.

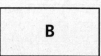

_____

11.

_____

12.

_____

13.

_____

14.

_____

15.

_____

16.

_____

17. Which figures look congruent?

_____

18. Which figures look as if their sides are parallel?

_____

19. Which figures look as if their sides are perpendicular?

_____

20. Which figures look as if their sides are both parallel and perpendicular?

_____

Perimeter and Area of Parallelograms

Name   **Date**

Homework

Find the perimeter and area of each complex figure.

1.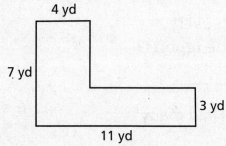

P = _____

A = _____

2.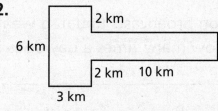

P = _____

A = _____

3.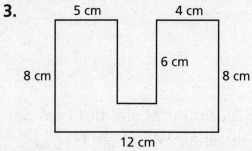

P = _____

A = _____

4.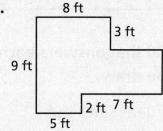

P = _____

A = _____

5. Draw a complex figure. Label the sides of
your figure and find its perimeter and area.

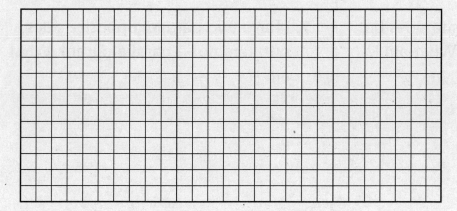

Remembering

Use the fact that there are 24 hours in a day to solve the word problems.

1. A TV station broadcasts updated weather reports every 3 hours. How many times a day does it update the reports?

   _____

2. Bob is sick and has to take 2 pills every 6 hours. How many pills will he take in a day?

   _____

3. A news website is updated 6 times a day. How many hours are there between updates?

   _____

Draw a quadrilateral that answers each riddle.
Name the figure you draw.

4. I have four congruent sides but I am not a square. What am I?

5. I have four right angles but I am not just a rectangle. What am I?

   _____   _____

6. I have parallel opposite sides but I am not a rectangle. What am I?

7. I have two parallel opposite sides but I am not a parallelogram. What am I?

   _____   _____

Homework

Write a number in each blank to make the equation or inequality true.

1. $9 + 2 = \underline{\hspace{1cm}} + 9$ **2.** $4 + \underline{\hspace{1cm}} \neq 13 - 6$ **3.** $4 = 8 - \underline{\hspace{1cm}} - 2$

4. $16 \neq 17 - \underline{\hspace{1cm}}$ **5.** $7 = \underline{\hspace{1cm}} - 8$ **6.** $5 + 7 \neq 25 - \underline{\hspace{1cm}}$

7. $\underline{\hspace{1cm}} + 3 = 31 - 20$ **8.** $13 - 5 \neq 1 + 7 + \underline{\hspace{1cm}}$ **9.** $d + 6 = \underline{\hspace{1cm}} + d$

Write = or ≠ to make each statement true.

10. $5 + 2 + 6 \bigcirc 6 + 7$ **11.** $90 \bigcirc 110 - 9$ **12.** $70 \bigcirc 30 + 30$

13. $70 \bigcirc 95 - 25$ **14.** $2 + 8 + 10 \bigcirc 30$ **15.** $27 - 10 \bigcirc 14 + 3$

16. $51 + 99 \bigcirc 150$ **17.** $35 \bigcirc 100 - 55$ **18.** $50 \bigcirc 20 + 5 + 20$

Use an inverse operation and solve for the unknown.

19. $70 = 20 + h$ **20.** $y + 60 = 90$ **21.** $100 - c = 10$

$h = \underline{\hspace{1.5cm}}$ $y = \underline{\hspace{1.5cm}}$ $c = \underline{\hspace{1.5cm}}$

22. $n - 7 = 3$ **23.** $5 = 9 - r$ **24.** $16 = e + 7$

$n = \underline{\hspace{1.5cm}}$ $r = \underline{\hspace{1.5cm}}$ $e = \underline{\hspace{1.5cm}}$

25. $s + 2 = 10$ **26.** $50 - k = 10$ **27.** $20 = 16 + m$

$s = \underline{\hspace{1.5cm}}$ $k = \underline{\hspace{1.5cm}}$ $m = \underline{\hspace{1.5cm}}$

28. Write the eight related addition and subtraction equations for the break-apart drawing.

   _____   _____

   _____   _____

   _____   _____

   _____   _____

Name _____   **Date** _____

Remembering

Complete.

1. _____ × 5 = 45   2. _____ ÷ 7 = 9   3. 8 × _____ = 40

4. 6)‾2‾4‾ = _____   5. 7 • _____ = 42   6. 30 ÷ 5 = _____

7. 5 • 5 = _____   8. 81 ÷ _____ = 9   9. 9 • _____ = 72

10. 14 ÷ _____ = 7   11. 7 × 9 = _____   12. 48 / 8 = _____

13. 3 × _____ = 24   14. 7)‾5‾6‾ = _____   15. _____ × 9 = 36

16. _____ ÷ 10 = 7   17. _____ • 8 = 48   18. 36 ÷ 4 = _____

Write all the factor pairs of each number.

19. 10 _____

20. 24 _____

Write and solve an equation for each problem.

21. Jon's mother made 27 party favors for his birthday. If 9 of his friends are invited to his party, how many party favors can each of his friends be given?

_____

_____

22. Each page of Sara's photo album contains 4 rows of pictures. If each page holds a total of 16 pictures, how many pictures can she place in each row?

_____

_____

23. Becky has one pair of black shoes and one pair of brown shoes. She wears one pair of shoes with one pair of colored socks everyday. She can choose from 8 different shoe and sock combinations. How many pairs of different colored socks does Becky have?

_____

_____

24. To prepare for a math test, Eric studied three times as long as Kendra and one-half as long as Gerardo. How long did Gerardo study if Kendra studied for 20 minutes?

_____

_____

Understand Equality

Homework

Solve each problem.   *Show your work.*

1. A teacher assigned 13 projects. Zack finished 5 of the projects early and 6 on time. How many projects did he finish late?

   _____

2. An electronics store offers 130 different video games for sale. This week, 90 of those games do not have a discounted price. How many games have a discounted price?

   _____

3. A red vase has 20 more flowers than a yellow vase. The yellow vase has 30 more flowers than a blue vase. There are 67 flowers in the blue vase. How many flowers are in the red vase?

   _____

4. To get ready for a test, Thomas studied for 35 minutes and Elena studied for 1 hour and 10 minutes. How many fewer minutes did Thomas study than Elena?

   _____

5. During the morning, 16 students shopped at the school bookstore. By the end of the afternoon, 23 students had shopped. How many fewer students shopped in the afternoon than in the morning?

   _____

6. A 64-page notebook contains 35 pages of science notes and 17 pages of math notes. Can the notebook also contain 10 pages of notes about other subjects? Explain why or why not.

   _____

Remembering

Complete.

1. _____ ÷ 9 = 7

2. 7 × _____ = 56

3. 8)‾4‾0‾ = _____

4. 6 • _____ = 24

5. 42 ÷ 7 = _____

6. 5 • 7 = _____

7. 21 ÷ _____ = 3

8. 9 × 6 = _____

9. 30 / 6 = _____

Simplify each expression.

10. 8 × (6 + 2) = _____

11. (8 × 6) + 2 = _____

12. 2 × 8 + 6 = _____

Solve.

13. $e - 9 = 8$

$e =$ _____

14. $t + 3 = 12$

$t =$ _____

15. $60 - g = 40$

$g =$ _____

16. $100 + 50 = j$

$j =$ _____

17. $11 - 5 = p$

$p =$ _____

18. $30 + i = 110$

$i =$ _____

Write = or ≠ to make each statement true.

19. 7 + 6 ◯ 15 − 3

20. 70 − 10 ◯ 40 + 40

21. 4 + 7 ◯ 13 − 2

22. 80 − 20 ◯ 10 + 50

23. 6 + 9 ◯ 10 − 5

24. 90 − 40 ◯ 20 + 20

25. Each unit square of the rectangles below represents
1 square inch. Name the rectangle that shows perimeter,
and name the perimeter. Then name the rectangle that
shows area, and name the area.

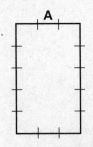 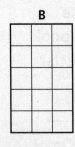

_____

_____

_____

_____

Name _____ **Date** _____

Homework

Solve.

Show your work.

1. Erin has red, blue, and yellow barrettes. She has 5 times as many blue barrettes as red barrettes, and 2 times as many yellow barrettes as red barrettes. Altogether, she has 24 barrettes. How many of each color does she have?

   _____

2. Each guest at a birthday party received 3 presents. Altogether, 24 presents were distributed to guests. How many guests attended the party?

   _____

3. A fish biologist counted 7 times as many perch as northern pike. The biologist counted 35 perch. How many northern pike did she count?

   _____

4. In a fifth-grade class of 16 students, one-half of the students arrived at school early, one-fourth of the students arrived on time, and one-eighth of the students arrived late. On that day, how many students were absent?

   _____

5. A stamp collector is arranging 100 stamps in rows with the same number of stamps in each row. How many different ways could she arrange the stamps if she would like more than 2 rows but fewer than 10 rows? Explain your answer.

   _____

   _____

   _____

   _____

Mixed Word Problems **95**

Name _____   **Date** _____

Remembering

Complete.

1. 9 × _____ = 63   **2.** 8)‾56‾ = _____   **3.** _____ ÷ 5 = 7

4. _____ • 9 = 72   **5.** 45 ÷ 9 = _____   **6.** 6 • 6 = _____

7. 36 ÷ _____ = 9   **8.** 10 × 7 = _____   **9.** _____ × 9 = 54

10. _____ ÷ 8 = 3   **11.** 4 × _____ = 32   **12.** 21 ÷ 3 = _____

Simplify each expression.

13. 7 × (4 − 2) = _____   **14.** (7 × 4) − 2 = _____   **15.** 14 ÷ (2 + 5) = _____

This graph shows the average weight in pounds of three types of sea turtles.

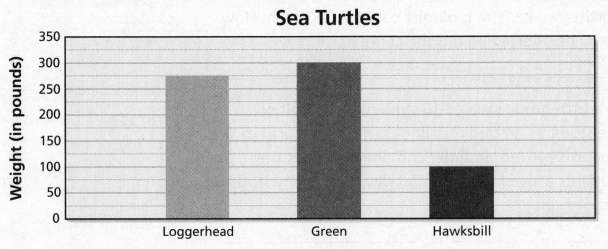

16. About how many more pounds does a loggerhead turtle weigh than a hawksbill?

_____

17. About how many more pounds does a green turtle weigh than a loggerhead?

_____

18. About how many times the weight of a hawksbill turtle is the weight of a green turtle?

_____

19. Four green turtles is about the same weight as what number of hawksbill turtles?

_____

Mixed Word Problems

Homework

Write the number of tens and the number of ones in each number.

1. 56

2. 708

3. 6,170

_____ tens   _____ tens   _____ tens

_____ ones   _____ ones   _____ ones

Write the number of thousands and the number of hundreds in each number.

4. 4,982

5. 316

6. 2,057

_____ thousands   _____ thousands   _____ thousands

_____ hundreds   _____ hundreds   _____ hundreds

Make a place-value drawing for each number, using ones, quick tens, hundred boxes, and thousand bars.

7. 36   **8.** 510

9. 403   **10.** 1,072

Name _____ **Date** _____

Remembering

Complete.

1. $8 \times$ _____ $= 56$ 2. $9\overline{)36} =$ _____ 3. $9 \cdot$ _____ $= 18$

4. $64 \div 8 =$ _____ 5. $4 \cdot 6 =$ _____ 6. $35 \div$ _____ $= 5$

7. $10 \cdot$ _____ $= 60$ 8. $28 \div$ _____ $= 7$ 9. $8 \times 5 =$ _____

10. $27 / 9 =$ _____ 11. $5 \times$ _____ $= 45$ 12. _____ $\times 7 = 49$

Simplify each expression.

13. $28 \div (4 + 3) =$ _____ 14. $(28 \div 4) + 3 =$ _____ 15. $28 - (4 \times 3) =$ _____

Write the perimeter (*P*) and the area (*A*) of each figure.

16.

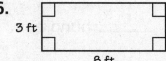

P = _____

A = _____

17.

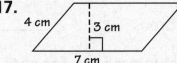

P = _____

A = _____

18.

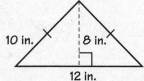

P = _____

A = _____

19.

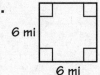

P = _____

A = _____

Write and solve an equation for each problem.

20. Paige read 10 books. This is 4 more books than Gina read. How many books did Gina read?

_____

_____

21. Dominique is 9 years old. She is 14 years younger than Nathaniel. How old is Nathaniel?

_____

_____

Place Value to Thousands

Homework

Write each number in standard form.

1. two hundred seventy-nine _____

2. three thousand, fifty-four _____

3. eight hundred two _____

4. nine thousand, one hundred _____

Round each number to the nearest ten.

5. 46 _____   **6.** 81 _____   **7.** 75 _____   **8.** 24 _____

Round each number to the nearest hundred.

9. 789 _____   **10.** 971 _____   **11.** 709 _____   **12.** 148 _____

Round each number to the nearest thousand.

13. 6,578 _____   **14.** 4,489 _____   **15.** 8,099 _____   **16.** 2,761 _____

Solve.

17. When you round a number, which digit in the number helps you decide to round up or round down? Explain your answer.

_____

_____

_____

_____

_____

18. When you round a number, what should you do with the digits to the right of the place you are rounding to?

_____

_____

_____

Remembering

Complete.

1. $9 \times$ _____ $= 45$

2. $4\overline{)32} =$ _____

3. _____ $\times 7 = 42$

4. _____ $\div 6 = 8$

5. _____ $\bullet 5 = 35$

6. $40 \div 5 =$ _____

7. $5 \bullet 6 =$ _____

8. $63 \div$ _____ $= 9$

9. $8 \bullet$ _____ $= 40$

10. $72 \div$ _____ $= 9$

11. $3 \times 8 =$ _____

12. $24 / 6 =$ _____

13. _____ $\div 3 = 9$

14. $8 \bullet$ _____ $= 56$

15. $12 \div 2 =$ _____

Simplify each expression.

16. $7 \times 8 - 6 =$ _____

17. $7 \times (8 - 6) =$ _____

18. $7 + 8 \times 6 =$ _____

Find the perimeter and area.

19.

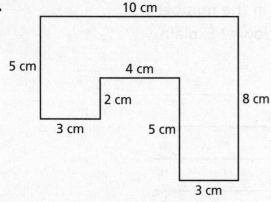

Perimeter: _____

Area: _____

Write and solve an equation for each problem.

20. In Kelsey's class, 4 students earned an A on an exam. In Jordan's class, 4 times as many students earned an A. How many more students earned an A in Jordan's class than in Kelsey's class?

_____

_____

21. Lorenzo has saved $6 for a new sweater. If he saves another dollar, he will have saved one-fourth of the amount he needs to purchase the sweater. What is the cost of the sweater?

_____

_____

Read, Write, and Round Numbers

Use the information in the table to answer the questions.

Driving Distances (in miles) between Various Cities in the United States

	New York, NY	Chicago, IL	Los Angeles, CA
Atlanta, GA	886	717	2,366
Dallas, TX	1,576	937	1,450
Nashville, TN	914	578	2,028
Omaha, NE	1,257	483	1,561
Seattle, WA	2,912	2,108	1,141
Wichita, KS	1,419	740	1,393

1. If you drove from New York to Dallas and then from Dallas to Chicago, how many miles would you have driven?

_____

2. Which two cities are farther apart in driving distance: Seattle and Los Angeles or Wichita and New York? Use place-value words to explain your answer.

_____

_____

3. José drove from Omaha to New York and from New York to Atlanta. Keesha drove from Nashville to Los Angeles. Did José or Keesha travel more miles? Use place-value words to explain your answer.

_____

_____

Use any method to add. On another sheet of paper, make a drawing for exercise 5 to show your new groups.

4. 653 + 908   **5.** 369 + 754   **6.** 262 + 746   **7.** 723 + 265

_____   _____   _____   _____

Name _____ **Date** _____

Remembering

Solve each problem.

Show your work.

1. Kai bought 12 rolls of paper towels at the grocery store. Each package contained 3 rolls. How many packages did he buy?

   _____

2. Mr. Chen used 18 cups of flour to bake cakes at his bakery. He used 2 cups for each cake. How many cakes did Mr. Chen bake?

   _____

3. Six teams entered a basketball tournament. Three teams had 10 players each, and each of the other teams had 9 players. How many players were in the tournament?

   _____

4. A rectangle has a length of 10 centimeters and an area of 40 square centimeters. What is the width of the rectangle?

   _____

5. The length of a rectangle is 2 inches more than its width. The area of the rectangle is 15 square inches. What are the length and width of the rectangle?

   _____

Compare. Write > (greater than) or < (less than).

6. 65 $\bigcirc$ 68

7. 345 $\bigcirc$ 354

8. 4,328 $\bigcirc$ 4,238

9. 87 $\bigcirc$ 77

10. 906 $\bigcirc$ 916

11. 13,156 $\bigcirc$ 12,561

12. 115 $\bigcirc$ 151

13. 1,543 $\bigcirc$ 1,453

14. 23,901 $\bigcirc$ 32,109

Make New Groups for Addition

Homework

Write a number sentence that shows an estimate of each answer. Then write the exact answer.

1. 69 + 25 _____

2. 259 + 43 _____

3. 2,009 + 995 _____

Solve.

4. Paul's stamp collection includes 192 domestic and 811 foreign stamps.

About how many domestic and foreign stamps does Paul have altogether?

_____

Exactly how many domestic and foreign stamps does Paul have altogether?

_____

Show your work.

5. Four family members visited a café. Bryn's chicken sandwich cost $5.75. Her sister's grilled cheese cost $4.25. Her grandfather's tuna sandwich cost $5.25, and her brother's turkey club cost $6.75.

About how much did the sandwiches cost altogether?

_____

Exactly how much did the sandwiches cost altogether?

_____

Drinks cost $6.50 and tax totaled $1.71. *Exactly* how much did the family spend?

_____

Remembering

Complete.

1. _____ × 6 = 48   2. _____ ÷ 4 = 8   3. 5 × _____ = 30

4. 9)$\overline{54}$ = _____   5. 9 • _____ = 81   6. 35 ÷ 5 = _____

7. 3 • 8 = _____   8. 27 ÷ _____ = 3   9. 10 • _____ = 50

10. 30 ÷ _____ = 5   11. 49 / 7 = _____   12. _____ × 6 = 42

Simplify each expression.

13. 22 ÷ 11 + 3 = _____   14. 8 × 4 − 6 = _____   15. 19 − (2 × 9) = _____

Round each number to the nearest ten and to the nearest hundred.

16. 773 _____

17. 5,197 _____

18. 16,349 _____

Circle the number that is closer in value to the underlined number.

19. <u>54</u> 65 or 45   20. <u>85</u> 92 or 72   21. <u>139</u> 125 or 155

22. <u>960</u> 950 or 975   23. <u>2,755</u> 1,755 or 2,955   24. <u>1,280</u> 1,260 or 1,290

25. Write the missing dimensions. Then write the perimeter (*P*) and the area (*A*) of the figure.

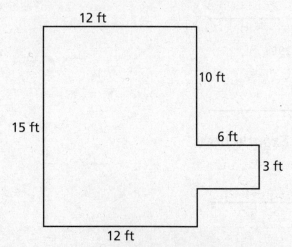

12 ft

10 ft

15 ft

6 ft

3 ft

12 ft

P = _____   *A* = _____

Estimation and Mental Math

**Subtract. On a separate sheet of paper, make a drawing
to show how you ungrouped and subtracted.**

1. 300 − 165 = _____   **2.** 500 − 348 = _____   **3.** 700 − 279 = _____

Solve.   *Show your work.*

4. LaShauna bought a 200-sheet package of construction
paper. Twenty-five of the sheets were red, 16 were
green, and the rest were other colors. How many
sheets were other colors?

_____

5. Mario brought a package of 100 cheese crackers to
share with his class. There are 33 students in Mario's
class. If each student is given 2 crackers, how many
crackers will not be eaten?

_____

6. The Summer Club is bike-riding for fun. Each rider's
goal is to ride 100 kilometers. During the first week
Jerry rode 18 kilometers, and Kim rode twice as far as
Jerry. How many more kilometers must Kim ride to
reach the goal?

_____

7. Sue Ann practices her violin for 200 minutes each
week. If she practices 25 minutes on Monday, on
Tuesday, and on Wednesday, how many minutes
does she need to practice the rest of the week?

_____

8. In a large backyard, there are 4 times as many shrubs
as trees. Altogether, there are 40 trees and shrubs.
How many trees are in the yard? How many shrubs?

_____

Remembering

Write and solve each multiplication or division as quickly as you can. Circle any that you did not know right away so that you can continue to practice them at home.

1. 3 • 9 = _____

2. 8 × 7 = _____

3. 2 • 7 = _____

4. 8 × 9 = _____

5. 7 * 7 = _____

6. 5 • 9 = _____

7. 8 * 8 = _____

8. 4 • 9 = _____

9. 6 × 7 = _____

10. 2 • 9 = _____

11. 6 × 9 = _____

12. 5 * 7 = _____

13. 25 ÷ 5 = _____

14. 12 / 3 = _____

15. 5)‾10‾ _____

16. 35 / 5 = _____

17. 3)‾24‾ _____

18. 45 ÷ 5 = _____

19. 3)‾6‾ _____

20. 30 ÷ 5 = _____

21. 21 / 3 = _____

22. 72 / 8 _____

23. 63 ÷ 7 = _____

24. 8)‾56‾ _____

Round each number to the nearest hundred and to the nearest thousand.

25. 54,158

26. 14,273

27. 21,844

28. 61,729

_____   _____   _____   _____

_____   _____   _____   _____

Each figure has one or more lines of symmetry. Use a ruler to draw the lines.

29.

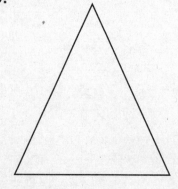

30.

31.

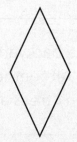

Homework

Subtract. Then write and solve an addition problem that checks the subtraction.

1. 400 − 238 = _____   **2.** 900 − 379 = _____   **3.** 700 − 462 = _____

Check: _____   Check: _____   Check: _____

Solve.

Show your work.

4. Keesha has 58 books in her collection. Daryl has 63 books. How many books do they have altogether?

_____

5. Daryl told his teacher the number of books he has, and the number of books he and Keesha have altogether. The teacher wanted to know how many books Keesha has. How can Daryl use subtraction to give the teacher an answer?

_____

6. The zoo keepers fed the penguins 79 fish in the morning and 86 fish in the afternoon. How many fish did they feed the penguins altogether?

_____

7. The head keeper knew how many fish the penguins had been fed altogether, and she knew they had been fed 86 fish in the afternoon. Write a subtraction number sentence to show how the keeper could determine the number of fish the penguins had been fed in the morning.

_____

8. Math Journal Write and solve a subtraction word problem. Use addition to check your subtraction.

Name _____ **Date** _____

Remembering

Complete.

1. _____ × 8 = 56

2. _____ ÷ 9 = 6

3. 7 × _____ = 49

4. 6⟌48 = _____

5. 8 • _____ = 72

6. 64 ÷ 8 = _____

Write the value of the underlined digit.

7. 8,5̲04 _____

8. 9̲8,715 _____

9. 39̲,785 _____

10. 4̲86,156 _____

11. 218,40̲1 _____

12. 6̲,748,166 _____

Use the graph to answer the questions that follow.

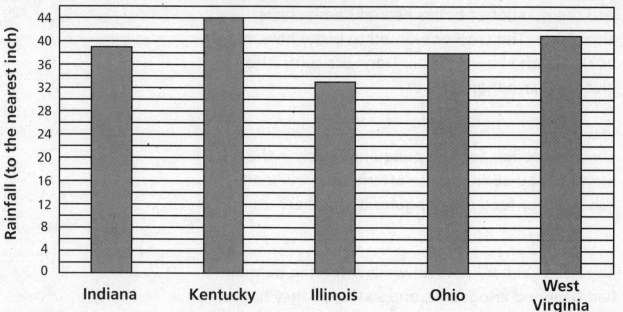

Average Annual Rainfall

13. Which state receives more average annual rainfall, West Virginia or Indiana?

_____

14. Which state receives an average of 6 fewer inches of rainfall than Kentucky?

_____

15. Which state or states receive more than 3 feet of rainfall annually?

_____

16. Which two states together receive an average of 6 feet of annual rainfall?

_____

Subtraction Undoes Addition

Homework

Subtract. Make a place-value drawing for each problem if you need to.

1. 621 − 488 = _____   **2.** 846 − 282 = _____   **3.** 735 − 217 = _____

Solve.

Show your work.

4. Susan found 329 pennies in a jar in the attic. She gave 175 of the pennies to her brother. How many pennies did she keep for herself?

_____

5. A group of students weighed potatoes for a science experiment. They found one potato had a mass of 346 grams and another had a mass of 278 grams. What is the difference in the mass of the two potatoes?

_____

6. Jeremy received a bag of marbles for his birthday. He counted 183 in all. He gave 85 to his best friend. How many marbles did Jeremy keep for himself?

_____

7. A four-floor apartment building is 40 feet tall. The ground floor is 11 feet tall, and the next two floors are each 9 feet tall. How tall is the fourth floor?

_____

8. Write and solve your own subtraction word problem. The greatest number in your problem should not include zeros.

_____

_____

_____

Remembering

Write and solve each multiplication or division as quickly as you can. Circle any that you did not know right away so that you can continue to practice them at home.

1. _____ ÷ 9 = 2

2. 7 × _____ = 42

3. 6)‾36 = _____

4. 4 • _____ = 32

5. 40 ÷ 8 = _____

6. 9 • 0 = _____

7. 72 ÷ _____ = 9

8. 9 • _____ = 63

9. 5 × 7 = _____

10. 30 / 10 = _____

11. 8 × _____ = 72

12. 4)‾28 = _____

13. _____ × 9 = 54

14. _____ ÷ 6 = 8

15. _____ • 7 = 56

Simplify each expression.

16. 4 + 12 × 3 = _____

17. 2 × (16 ÷ 4) = _____

18. 5 × 5 ÷ 5 = _____

19. 24 ÷ (6 − 3) = _____

20. 9 × 6 − 4 = _____

21. 27 − 5 × 4 = _____

22. Write a general description about how to round numbers.

_____

_____

_____

_____

23. Circle all the congruent triangles.

24. Explain why the triangles you circled are congruent.

_____

_____

_____

Ungroup for Any Subtraction

Subtract. Show your new groups.

1. 7,000
    − 3,264

2. 9,632
    − 3,785

3. 8,054
    − 1,867

4. 6,478 − 3,579 = _____ 5. 9,490 − 5,512 = _____ 6. 5,000 − 3,609 = _____

Solve.

Show your work.

7. A cross-country automobile rally is 1,025 kilometers long. At a stopping place, the leader had traveled 867 kilometers. How far away was the finish line?

_____

8. A census counted 5,407 people in Marina's home town. If 3,589 are males, how many are females?

_____

9. A construction company is building a stone wall. The finished wall will contain 5,000 stones. So far, 1,487 stones have been placed. How many stones have not been placed?

_____

10. Jake has 647 pennies in his penny collection album. The album has space for 1,000 pennies. How many more pennies can Jake place in his album?

_____

11. Write and solve a multi-digit subtraction word problem.

_____

_____

_____

_____

Remembering

Write and solve each multiplication or division as quickly as you can. Circle any that you did not know right away so that you can continue to practice them at home.

1. $9 \cdot 6 =$ _____

2. $4 \times 8 =$ _____

3. $5 * 6 =$ _____

4. $8 \cdot 8 =$ _____

5. $3 \times 6 =$ _____

6. $1 * 8 =$ _____

7. $7 \cdot 6 =$ _____

8. $5 \times 8 =$ _____

9. $7 \cdot 8 =$ _____

10. $36 \div 9 =$ _____

11. $63 / 7 =$ _____

12. $9\overline{)18}$ _____

13. $35 \div 7 =$ _____

14. $81 / 9 =$ _____

15. $7\overline{)49}$ _____

16. $9 \div 9 =$ _____

17. $21 / 7 =$ _____

18. $6\overline{)42}$ _____

Add. Estimate to check.

19. $90,206 + 83,987 =$

_____

20. $12,098 + 92,312 =$

_____

21. $354,435 + 86,210 =$

_____

22. $462,111 + 867,241 =$

_____

Solve.

Show your work.

23. A rectangle has a perimeter of 60 cm. Its length is 5 times greater than its width. What is its length?

_____

24. The perimeter of a triangle is 30 inches. The first side of the triangle is 1 inch longer than the second side. The second side is 7 inches longer than the third side. What is the length of each side of the triangle?

_____

Subtract.

1. 71,824 − 36,739 = _____

2. 1,660,739 − 894,045 = _____

3. 56,065,717 − 5,682,824 = _____

4. 372,608 − 57,425 = _____

5. 4,597,603 − 704,980 = _____

6. 9,614,702 − 539,508 = _____

7. 724,359 − 99,068 = _____

8. 394,280 − 56,473 = _____

In 1990 there were about 33,000,000 people living in the Great Lakes basin. The table shows how the people were distributed.

Lake	Population
Erie	11,682,169
Huron	2,694,154
Michigan	10,057,026
Ontario	8,150,895
Superior	607,121

Solve. Estimate to check.

Show your work.

9. What was the difference between the greatest population and the least population?

_____

10. How many more people lived in the Lake Ontario region than in the Lake Huron region?

_____

11. How many fewer people lived in the Lake Michigan region than in the combined regions of Lake Huron and Lake Ontario?

_____

Remembering

Write and solve each multiplication or division as quickly as you can. Circle any that you did not know right away so that you can continue to practice them at home.

1. $4 \times$ _____ $= 16$

2. $7\overline{)42} =$ _____

3. _____ $\times 6 = 24$

4. _____ $\div 3 = 7$

5. _____ $\bullet 5 = 35$

6. $9\overline{)63} =$ _____

7. $5 \bullet 8 =$ _____

8. 48 _____ $= 6$

9. 9 _____ $= 72$

10. 12 _____ $= 3$

11. $1 \times 7 =$ _____

12. $56 / 7 =$ _____

13. _____ $\times 9 = 81$

14. _____ $\div 9 = 6$

15. 3 _____ $= 24$

Solve.   *Show your work.*

16. Shawn sold 9 fundraiser tickets. Trina sold 3 times as many tickets as Shawn. How many tickets did Trina sell?

_____

17. A vendor sells 6 roses for $4. At that rate, what is the cost of 2 dozen roses? (1 dozen = 12)

_____

18. Look at the shapes below.

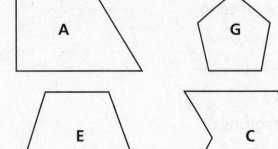

Write the letters for the shapes that are quadrilaterals. _____

Homework

This table shows the area in square miles of the five largest islands of the world. Use the data to answer the questions.

Island	Location	Area (square miles)
Baffin	North Atlantic Ocean	195,928
Borneo	Pacific Ocean	285,000
Greenland	North Atlantic Ocean	840,000
Madagascar	Indian Ocean	226,658
New Guinea	Pacific Ocean	305,000

Solve.

Show your work.

1. Estimate the total area of the islands in the table that are located in the North Atlantic Ocean. Explain your thinking.

   _____

   _____

2. Which is greater: The area of the largest island, or an estimate of the sum of the areas of the next four largest islands? Explain your thinking.

   _____

   _____

   _____

Estimate each sum or difference by rounding each number to the nearest hundred. Then write the exact answer.

3. 321 + 888

   _____

   _____

4. 1,617 − 514

   _____

   _____

5. 3,997 + 2,013

   _____

   _____

Remembering

Add or subtract. Show your work on a separate sheet of paper.

1. 1,286,360 − 942,207 = _____

2. 19,280 + 23,521,888 = _____

Solve.

Show your work.

3. Blaine has $6.00. He wants to buy action figures that cost $1.95 each. How many action figures can he buy?

_____

4. Teresa needs to buy a hat. She also wants to buy gloves for her sister. A hat costs $4.80 and gloves cost $3.25. Teresa has $9.00. Does she have enough money?

_____

5. Regina has $10.00. She wants to buy a key chain that costs $2.40 and a book that costs $7.95. Does she have enough money to buy both?

_____

6. Bill has 2 hours until bedtime. He needs to spend 30 minutes practicing his trumpet and 30 minutes doing math homework. Then he can read his book. How long can Bill read before bedtime?

_____

7. Write the missing dimensions. Then write the perimeter (*P*) and area (*A*).

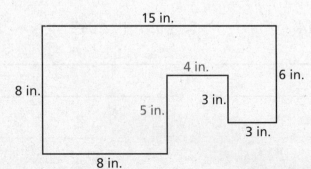

P = _____   A = _____

Estimate With Real-World Situations

Add or subtract.

1. 12,673 − 9,717 = _____   **2.** 8,406 + 45,286 = _____   **3.** 2,601 − 1,437 = _____

Answer each question about the information in the table.

Area of the Countries of Central America

Country	Area (square miles)
Belize	8,867
Costa Rica	19,730
El Salvador	8,124
Guatemala	42,042
Honduras	43,278
Nicaragua	49,998
Panama	30,193

4. Which country has a greater area: Guatemala or Honduras? Use place-value words to explain your thinking.

Show your work.

_____

_____

_____

5. What is the total area of Guatemala and Honduras?

_____

6. Which two countries have the least area? What is the sum of their areas?

_____

7. Which is greater: the area of Nicaragua or the total area of Costa Rica and Panama?

_____

Name _____ **Date** _____

Remembering

Subtract. Then write and solve an addition problem to check your answer.

1. 500 − 329 = _____

Check: _____

2. 700 − 677 = _____

Check: _____

3. 300 − 168 = _____

Check: _____

Solve.

Show your work.

4. Bryant has 347 baseball cards. His brother has 109 more cards. How many cards does Bryant's brother have?

_____

5. Cheryl read a book that had 292 pages. Tonia read a book that had 436 pages. How many more pages did Tonia read?

_____

6. A bag of flower seeds contains 413 seeds. If 380 seeds grew into flowers, how many seeds did not grow?

_____

Does each figure have at least one line of symmetry? Write _yes_ or _no_.

7.  _____

8. 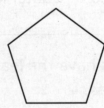 _____

9. 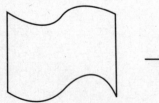 _____

10.  _____

Problem Solving With Larger Numbers

Homework

1. Connections

Ms. Martinez bought 52 red apples and 39 green apples at the store. She gave away 28 green apples. How many apples did she have left? Explain how you solved the problem.

_____

_____

_____

_____

2. Reasoning and Proof

Support or disprove the following statement with examples.

If Shape A is congruent to Shape B, and Shape B is congruent to Shape C, then Shape A is congruent to Shape C.

_____

_____

_____

3. Communication

A newspaper reporter wanted to report the number of people who went to a state fair. The actual number was 48,791 people. The newspaper reporter wants to use a rounded number. What number do you think she should use? Why?

_____

_____

_____

4. Representation

Use pictures to show that 1,456 and 4,615 have different values. Explain how the pictures show that the values are different.

_____

_____

_____

Name _____   **Date** _____

Remembering

Add or subtract. Show your work on a separate sheet of paper.

1. 1,784,326 − 875,158 = _____   **2.** 25,764 + 42,788,154 = _____

Solve.

3. Carlos has $12.00. He wants to buy notebooks   *Show your work.*
that cost $3.95 each. How many notebooks
can he buy?

_____

4. Tori wants to buy a book that costs $5.70 and
a set of stickers that costs $2.60. She has $8.00.
Does she have enough money?

_____

5. Otis has $9.00. He wants to buy model cars that
cost $1.50 each. How many model cars can he buy?

_____

Does each figure have at least one line of symmetry?
Write *yes* or *no*.

6.

_____

7.

_____

8.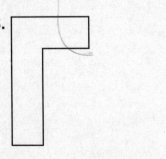

_____

9.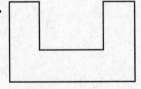

_____

Write the geometric name for each figure.

1.

_____

2.

_____

3.

_____

4.

_____

5.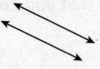

_____

6.

_____

Use a protractor to measure the angle.

7.

_____

8.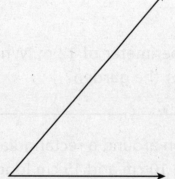

_____

9.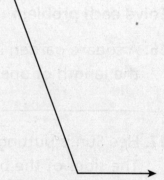

_____

10. Draw two examples of a line, a line segment, and a ray.

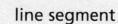

line   line segment   ray

Remembering

**Solve each division as quickly as you can. Circle any
that you didn't know right away so that you can
practice them at home.**

1. $18 \div 2 =$ ___   **2.** $4\overline{)4}$ **3.** $14 / 2 =$ ___   **4.** $24 \div 8 =$ ___

5. $42 / 7 =$ ___   **6.** $35 \div 7 =$ ___   **7.** $3\overline{)30}$ **8.** $48 / 6 =$ ___

9. $5\overline{)10}$ **10.** $72 / 9 =$ ___   **11.** $49 \div 7 =$ ___   **12.** $8\overline{)64}$

**Use what you know about Addition Properties
to find the missing number.**

13. $302 + 65 =$ ___ $+ 302$ **14.** $(3 + 2) + 5 =$ ___ $+ (2 + 5)$ **15.** $4 + a = a +$ ___

Solve each problem.

Show your work.

16. A square garden has a perimeter of 12 m. What is
the length of one side of the garden?

_____

17. Hee Sun is putting ribbon around a rectangular box.
The sides of the box are 10 cm and 15 cm long.
What is the minimum length of ribbon she needs?

_____

18. Mr. Julio is putting outdoor carpeting on his patio.
The patio is 6 m long and 4 m wide. How much
carpeting does Mr. Julio need?

_____

19. Alec is putting trim around a bulletin board.
The bulletin board is 2 m long and 1 m wide.
What is the minimum length of trim he needs?

_____

Name Angles

1. Circle the answer choice that shows the arrow after a 90° clockwise turn.

a.   b.   c.

2. Circle the answer choice that shows the figure after a 180° counter-clockwise turn.

a. 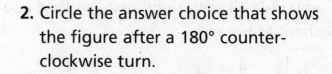   b.   c.

3. Circle the answer choice that shows the figure after a 90° counter-clockwise turn.

a.   b.   c.

4. Circle the answer choice that shows the figure after a 360° turn.

a. 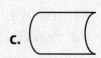   b.   c.

Does each figure have rotational symmetry? Write *yes* or *no*. If a figure has rotational symmetry, write the number of degrees of the rotation.

5.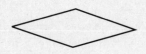

_____

6.

_____

7.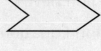

_____

Remembering

Solve each division as quickly as you can. Circle any that you didn't know right away so that you can practice them at home.

1. $16 \div 4 =$ _____   **2.** $1\overline{)5}$ _____   **3.** $27 / 9 =$ _____

4. $0 \div 5 =$ _____   **5.** $11\overline{)77} =$ _____   **6.** $81 / 9 =$ _____

7. $48 \div 12 =$ _____   **8.** $3\overline{)18} =$ _____   **9.** $36 / 4 =$ _____

10. $80 \div 10 =$ _____   **11.** $4\overline{)28} =$ _____   **12.** $90 / 10 =$ _____

Simplify each expression.

13. $7 + (9 \cdot 6) =$ _____   **14.** $(15 - 9) \times 5 =$ _____

15. $(8 - 5) \times (4 + 3) =$ _____   **16.** $16 \div 2 \times 8 =$ _____

Write a situation and a solution equation, using a letter to represent the unknown. Solve your equations.

17. Joe is placing bottles of juice on a shelf in a store. The shelf is deep enough to hold 4 bottles. If Joe has 48 bottles of juice, how many rows can he make?

Situation Equation: _____

Solution Equation: _____

18. Mrs. Pelz has 6 times as many teacups as Ms. Quinn. If Mrs. Pelz has 54 teacups, how many teacups does Ms. Quinn have?

Situation Equation: _____

Solution Equation: _____

19. Thirty-three cats are registered for a show. Before the show, the cats will stay in rows of cages that are stacked 3 high. How many cages will be in each row?

Situation Equation: _____

Solution Equation: _____

Name each triangle by its angles and then by its sides.

1.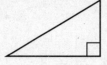

_____

_____

2.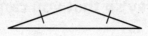

_____

_____

3.

_____

_____

4.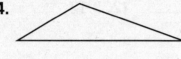

_____

_____

5.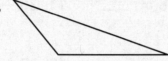

_____

_____

6.

_____

_____

7.

_____

_____

8.

_____

_____

9.

_____

_____

10. Describe how acute, obtuse, and right triangles are different.

_____

_____

_____

11. Describe how scalene, isosceles, and equilateral triangles are different.

_____

_____

_____

Remembering

Solve each division as quickly as you can. Circle any that you didn't know right away so that you can practice them at home.

1. $18 \div 9 =$ ___   2. $6\overline{)6}$ 3. $14 / 7 =$ ___   4. $24 \div 3 =$ ___

5. $42 / 6 =$ ___   6. $35 \div 5 =$ ___   7. $10\overline{)30}$ 8. $48 / 8 =$ ___

9. $2\overline{)10}$ 10. $72 / 8 =$ ___   11. $20 \div 4 =$ ___   12. $3\overline{)12}$

13. $25 \div 5 =$ ___   14. $1\overline{)7}$ 15. $27 / 3 =$ ___   16. $0 \div 7 =$ ___

Compare. Write = or ≠ to make each statement true.

17. $9 + 2 + 5 \bigcirc 4 \times 5$ 18. $6 \times 12 \bigcirc 8 \times 9$ 19. $5 \times 8 \bigcirc 7 \times 7 - 9$

Solve each problem.

Show your work.

20. Jessica wants to cover the top of a box with fabric. The box is 9 cm long and 8 cm wide. How much fabric does she need?

_____

21. A square carpet has an area of 9 square meters. What is the length of one side of the carpet?

_____

22. A quilt is 3 m long and 2 m wide. How many 1-meter squares were used to make the quilt?

_____

23. Henry wants to paint his closet door. The door is 2 m long and 1 m wide. What is the area of the closet door?

_____

Name Triangles

Homework

1. Draw a rectangle and a parallelogram. Draw one diagonal on each figure. Name the kinds of triangles you made.

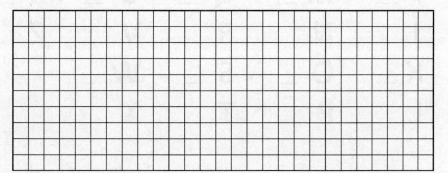

_____

_____

2. Draw your figures again. Draw the other diagonal and name the kinds of triangles you made this time.

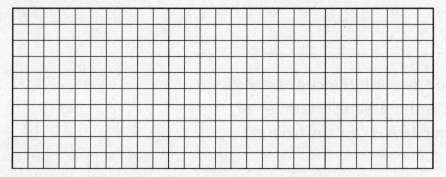

_____

_____

3. Use geometry words to describe how diagonals of quadrilaterals make triangles.

_____

_____

_____

_____

4. Use geometry words to describe how to join triangles to make quadrilaterals.

_____

_____

_____

_____

Remembering

1. Beside each letter tell how many lines of symmetry it has.

A __ E __ I __ M __ Q __ U __ Y __

B __ F __ J __ N __ R __ V __ Z __

C __ G __ K __ O __ S __ W __

D __ H __ L __ P __ T __ X __

Solve each problem.

Show your work.

2. Arturo took 9 pencils out of a box. Then there were 5 pencils left in the box. How many pencils were in the box to start with?

_____

3. A sheet of construction paper is 9 inches across and 11 inches high. What is the greatest number of 1-inch squares of paper James can cut from it?

_____

4. Zenaida lives 3 blocks from school. How many blocks does she walk to and from school from Monday through Friday?

_____

5. Sofia has a rug that is 6 feet long and 9 feet wide. Her room measures 8 feet each way. Will the rug fit in her room? How do you know?

_____

6. Hank's birthday is 2 days after Farha's. If it is 5 days until Farha's birthday, how many days is it until Hank's birthday?

_____

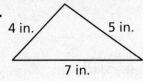

Name _____ **Date** _____

Find the perimeter.

1.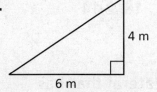

4 in.   5 in.

7 in.

_____

2.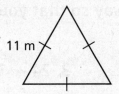

11 m

_____

3.

10 cm

6 cm

_____

Find the area.

4.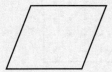

4 m

6 m

_____
_____

5.

8 cm

6 cm

_____
_____

6.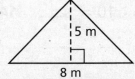

5 m

8 m

_____
_____

When you find the area of the figure, do you multiply by $\frac{1}{2}$? Write *yes* or *no*.

7.

_____

8.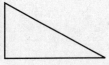

_____

9.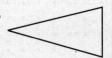

_____

Solve each problem.

Show your work.

10. Ben made a triangle-shaped dog pen that was 6 meters on each side. How much fencing did he need to enclose the dog pen on all sides?

_____

11. A sheet of paper measures 10 inches by 6 inches. Janie cut it on a diagonal into two congruent triangles. What is the area of each triangle?

_____

Remembering

Solve each of the following as quickly as you can. Circle any that you didn't know right away so that you can practice them at home.

1. 2 • 0 = ____ **2.** 5 * 4 = ____ **3.** 24 ÷ 3 = ____ **4.** 3)‾15‾

5. 3 × 1 = ____ **6.** 1 • 10 = ____ **7.** 100 / 10 = ____ **8.** 20 ÷ 10 = ____

9. 9 * 5 = ____ **10.** 6 × 2 = ____ **11.** 1)‾4‾ **12.** 9 / 9 = ____

13. 8 • 10 = ____ **14.** 7 * 3 = ____ **15.** 36 ÷ 4 = ____ **16.** 2)‾14‾

17. Draw a quadrilateral with no parallel sides.

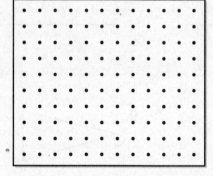

18. Draw a quadrilateral that has exactly two perpendicular sides.

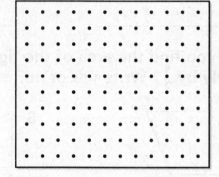

19. Draw a parallelogram. Explain why it is a parallelogram.

_____

_____

_____

_____

_____

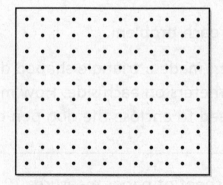

Perimeter and Area of Triangles

Name _____ **Date** _____

Homework

Name the polygon and write how many sides it has.

1.
_____

2.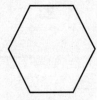
_____

3.
_____

4.
_____

5.
_____

6.
_____

7.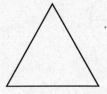
_____

8.
_____

9.
_____

10. All of the polygons above are regular polygons.
Write how to find the perimeter of polygon number 3.

_____

_____

What is the total perimeter of each group of regular polygons?

11.

6 ft   6 ft   6 ft

_____

12.

9 in.   9 in.   4 in.   4 in.

_____

13.

28 m   28 m   12 m

_____

14.

39 cm   19 cm   35 cm   26 cm

_____

Name _____ **Date** _____

Remembering

Use a protractor to measure the angle.

1.

2.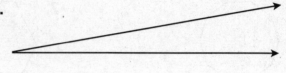

_____   _____

**Does each figure have rotational symmetry? Write *yes* or *no*.
If a figure has rotational symmetry, write the number of degrees of the rotation.**

3.    **4.**   **5.**

_____   _____   _____

Solve.   *Show your work.*

6. Maurice made a rectangle by putting together two 5-cm squares. What is the perimeter of his rectangle?

_____

7. Sheila drew some 3-cm squares and some 2-cm squares. The total area of all her squares was 35 sq cm. How many squares of each size did she draw?

_____

8. Write and solve an area or perimeter problem.

_____

_____

_____

_____

Homework

Which transformation is shown? Write *reflection*, *translation*, or *rotation*.

1.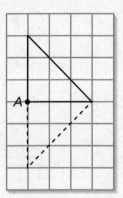

2.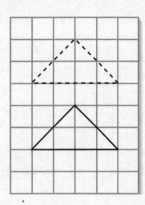

3.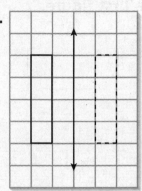

_____   _____   _____

Follow the directions.

4. Circle the figure that shows a 180° rotation of the first figure around Point *B*.

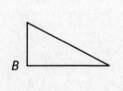 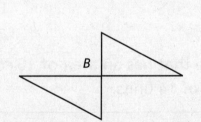 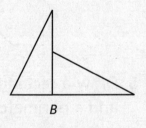

5. Draw a rectangle on the grid. Then show how to reflect it over a line.

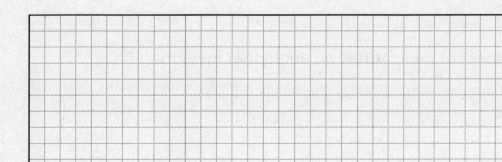

Remembering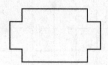

Circle the answer choice that appears to be similar to the first figure.

1.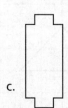

     a.   b.   c.

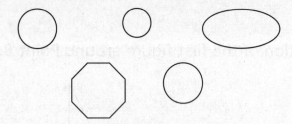

2.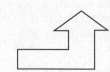

     a.    b.    c.

Circle the figures that appear to be congruent.

3.   4.

5. Draw a rectangle that has an area of 10 square units and a perimeter of 14 units.

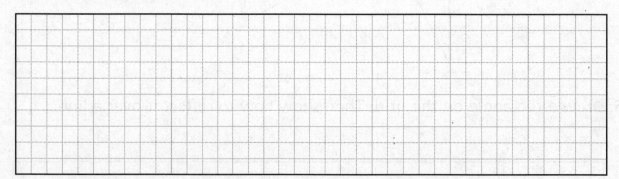

6. On a separate sheet of paper, draw an angle that measures 60°.

Estimate each product. Solve to check your estimate.

1. 4 × 26

_____

_____

2. 5 × 63

_____

_____

3. 7 × 95

_____

_____

4. 4 × 84

_____

_____

5. 2 × 92

_____

_____

6. 3 × 76

_____

_____

Estimate the answers. Then solve each problem.

Show your work.

7. Tony's little sister read 65 pages for the Summer Reading Club. Tony read 8 times as many pages as his sister. How many pages did Tony read?

_____

8. The school fair committee is making clown costumes. They found 23 different wigs and 9 different noses in the storeroom. How many different combinations are possible?

_____

9. The school library shows one book and one magazine each day in the display case. If the librarian has 37 books and 7 magazines to use for the display, how many days can a different pair be on display?

_____

Write and solve a multiplication word problem.

10. _____

_____

_____

Remembering

Use mental math to find each quotient.

1. $2\overline{)16}$ 2. $9\overline{)27}$ 3. $10\overline{)60}$

4. $4 \div 4 =$ _____   5. $30 \div 5 =$ _____   6. $20 \div 1 =$ _____

7. $\frac{14}{2} =$ _____   8. $\frac{0}{4} =$ _____   9. $\frac{15}{3} =$ _____

Classify each triangle according to its angles and sides.

10.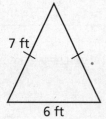

11.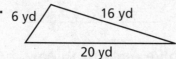

12.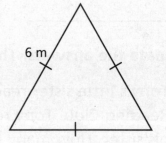

_____   _____   _____

Does each figure have at least one line of symmetry? Write *yes* or *no*.

13.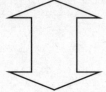

14.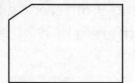

15.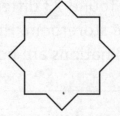

_____   _____   _____

Solve each problem.   *Show your work.*

16. A family is driving 330 miles to a state park. They have already driven 148 miles. How many more miles will they drive to reach the park?

_____

17. In an election, 7,285 people voted to build a city swimming pool, and 6,122 people voted against the plan. How many people voted?

_____

            Estimate Products

Homework

Sketch rectangles and solve by any method that relates to your sketch.

1. 3 × 687 _____

2. 8 × 572 _____

3. 5 × 919 _____

4. 6 × 458 _____

5. The soccer season lasts for 9 weeks. Lavonne's team practices 45 minutes on Saturdays. Jason's team practices 25 minutes on Mondays and on Thursdays. Which team practices more each week? How many more minutes do they practice during the season?

_____

Show your work.

6. Susie's grandmother lives about 800 miles away from her. Her mother's car can go about 350 miles on one tank of gasoline. How many times will Susie's mother have to fill the gas tank in order to drive to and from her grandmother's house?

_____

7. Zack has 42 basketball cards in his collection. Morry has 7 times as many cards as Zack. How many basketball cards do Zack and Morry have together?

_____

8. Write and solve a multiplication word problem with a three-digit number.

_____

_____

_____

Name _____ **Date** _____

Remembering

Use mental math to find each product.

1. $3 \cdot 3 =$ _____

2. $6 \cdot 6 =$ _____

3. $12 \cdot 12 =$ _____

4. $5 \times 5 =$ _____

5. $10 \times 12 =$ _____

6. $7 \times 7 =$ _____

7. $11 * 11 =$ _____

8. $8 * 8 =$ _____

9. $12 * 11 =$ _____

Find the perimeter and area of each figure.

10.

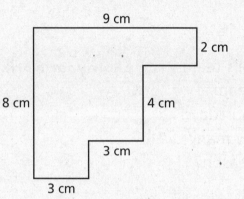

11.

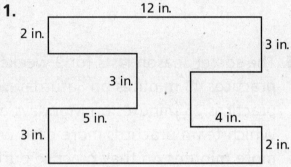

$P =$ _____ $A =$ _____

$P =$ _____ $A =$ _____

Solve each problem.

Show your work.

12. The soccer league has 96 players. If an equal number of players are put on 12 teams, how many players are on each team?

_____

13. The flower shop has 63 red tulips. If the florist uses these tulips to make bouquets containing 9 tulips, how many bouquets can she make?

_____

14. Write and solve a division word problem.

_____

_____

_____

One-Digit by Three-Digit Multiplication

Name _____ **Date** _____

On a separate sheet of paper, sketch a rectangle for each problem and solve, using any method. Round and estimate to check your answer.

1. 5×475 _____

2. 7×60 _____

3. 6×521 _____

4. 8×386 _____

5. Describe the steps you used for one of your solutions to exercises 1–4.

_____

_____

A fourth-grade class is counting the supplies in their art cupboard. Help them to finish their count.

Show your work.

6. They have 2 rolls of white craft paper. The paper on the rolls is 4 feet wide and 72 feet long. How many square feet of craft paper do they have altogether?

_____

7. They counted 88 boxes of colored pencils and 63 boxes of markers. If each box holds 8 pencils or markers, how many colored pencils and markers do they have altogether?

_____

8. They found 9 boxes of glass beads. There are 376 beads per box. How many glass beads do they have in all?

_____

9. They found 23 full pads of sketching paper and another 64 loose sheets. If each full pad has 90 sheets of paper, how many sheets of sketching paper do they have in all?

_____

Remembering

Compare each pair of numbers, using the greater than (>) or less than (<) sign.

1. 45 ____ 54

2. 574 ____ 754

3. 232,164 ____ 232,614

4. 3,889 ____ 3,898

5. 91,009 ____ 90,900

6. 810,001 ____ 809,999

Simplify each expression.

7. $9 \times 6 + 2 =$ _____

8. $9 \times (6 + 2) =$ _____

9. $9 + 6 \times 2 =$ _____

Find the area of each triangle.

10.

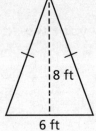

8 ft

6 ft

11.

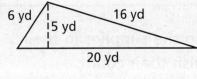

6 yd   5 yd   16 yd

20 yd

12.

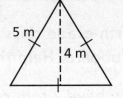

5 m   4 m

_____   _____   _____

Solve each problem.

Show your work.

13. Jacob has collected 186 baseball cards. Aimee has collected 152 cards. How many cards have they collected in all?

_____

14. If you drove 740 miles from Wichita, Kansas, to Chicago, Illinois, and then drove 578 more miles to Nashville, Tennessee, how many miles would you have driven?

_____

15. Write and solve an addition word problem.

_____

_____

_____

Practice One-Digit by Three-Digit Multiplication

Name _____ **Date** _____

Cross out the extra numerical information and solve. *Show your work.*

1. A gymnastic meet is 2 hours long. It has 8 competitors and each competes in 4 events. How many events will be scored?

   _____

2. George makes $20 doing lawn work for 4 hours each week. He wants to buy a $2,500 used car from his grandmother. He has been saving this money for 30 weeks. How much has he saved?

   _____

3. The fourth grade is raising money by selling roses for $2 a piece. Yesterday they paid $100 for 400 roses and sold 137 roses. How many roses are left?

   _____

Tell what additional information is needed to solve the problem.

4. Michelle is saving $20 each week for the bike of her dreams. How long until she can purchase her bike?

   _____

5. A teacher sees a sale on packages of pencils. She wants to give each of her students a pencil. How many packages should she buy?

   _____

   _____

6. Create a problem similar to exercise 4 or 5, but include the missing information.

   _____

   _____

   _____

Too Much or Too Little Information **157**

Name _____   **Date** _____

Remembering

Find the product.

1. $2 \times 65 =$ _____

2. $7 \times 39 =$ _____

3. $5 \times 82 =$ _____

4. $8 \times 48 =$ _____

5. $3 \times 16 =$ _____

6. $9 \times 57 =$ _____

7. $6 \times 91 =$ _____

8. $8 \times 74 =$ _____

9. $4 \times 23 =$ _____

Find the perimeter and area of each figure.

10.

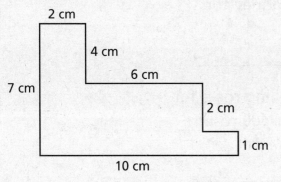

2 cm / 4 cm / 6 cm / 7 cm / 2 cm / 1 cm / 10 cm

11.

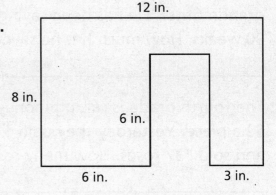

12 in. / 8 in. / 6 in. / 6 in. / 3 in.

$P =$ _____ $A =$ _____

$P =$ _____ $A =$ _____

Solve each problem.

Show your work.

12. An elementary school has 402 students. There are 197 boys that attend the school. How many girls attend the school?

_____

13. Natalie is reading a 216-page book. She has read 159 pages. How many more pages does she have to read?

_____

14. Write and solve a subtraction word problem.

_____

_____

_____

Too Much or Too Little Information

Name _____   Date _____

Solve each problem and label your answer.   *Show your work.*
Write hidden questions if you need to.

1. The school office prints a newsletter every month
   that uses 2 pieces of paper. They make 35 copies for
   each room. How many pieces of paper do they need
   to print copies for 10 rooms?

   _____

   _____

   _____

2. There are 18 windows on each side of a rectangular
   building. It takes the window washer 3 minutes to
   wash each window. How many minutes will it take
   to finish the job?

   _____

   _____

   _____

3. There are 34 parking spaces on each block of Main
   Street and another 94 spaces in the village lot. How
   many parking spaces are there on all 6 blocks of
   Main Street and in the lot?

   _____

   _____

   _____

Name _____ **Date** _____

Remembering

Use mental math to find each quotient.

1. $7\overline{)49}$

2. $12\overline{)132}$

3. $12\overline{)84}$

4. $88 \div 8 =$ _____

5. $25 \div 5 =$ _____

6. $81 \div 9 =$ _____

7. $\frac{36}{12} =$ _____

8. $\frac{96}{12} =$ _____

9. $\frac{55}{11} =$ _____

Identify the number of acute, obstuse, and right angles in each figure.

10.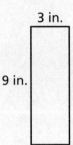

3 in.

9 in.

_____

11.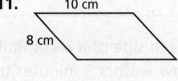

10 cm

8 cm

_____

12.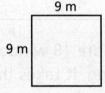

9 m

9 m

_____

Solve each problem. Show your work.

Show your work.

13. Mary has 143 shells and Casey has 86 shells. How many more shells does Mary have than Casey?

_____

14. Martin has 3 times as many baseball cards as Brad. Brad has 90 baseball cards. How many does Martin have?

_____

15. Write and solve a comparison word problem.

_____

_____

_____

_____

Solve MultiStep Word Problems

Homework

Multiply, using any method. If you use an area model to multiply, show your sketch.

1. 45 × 79   **2.** 88 × 29   **3.** 74 × 57   **4.** 84 × 68

_____   _____   _____   _____

Mr. Gomez's class is learning about multiplication. The class wants to see what multiplications they can find in their school. Solve each problem.

5. The class counts 37 tiles across the front of their room and 64 tiles down one side. How many floor tiles are in their classroom?

_____

6. The back of their classroom is a brick wall. Down one side, they count 26 rows of bricks. Across the bottom, they count 29 bricks. How many bricks make up the wall?

_____

7. In the school, there are 3 classrooms for each grade: kindergarten, 1, 2, 3, 4, 5, and 6. Each classroom has 32 lockers. How many lockers are there in the school building?

_____

8. The school auditorium has 69 rows of seats. Each row has 48 seats across. If 6,000 people want to see the school talent show, how many times do the students have to do the show?

_____

Write two multiplication word problems of your own. Then solve each problem.

9. _____

_____

_____

_____

10. _____

_____

_____

_____

Name _____ **Date** _____

Remembering

Find the product.

1. $6 \times 250 =$ _____

2. $4 \times 380 =$ _____

3. $7 \times 640 =$ _____

4. $275 \times 8 =$ _____

Classify each triangle according to its angles and sides.

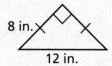

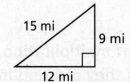

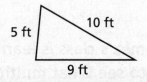

5. _____

6. _____

7. _____

Use a protractor to draw the angle on a separate sheet of paper.

8. a 40° angle

9. a 130° angle

10. a 180° angle

_____ _____ _____

Solve each problem.

Show your work.

11. George has 600 baseball cards. Joycelyn has one fifth as many baseball cards as George. How many baseball cards does Joycelyn have?

_____

12. Dawn has decided to read twice as much as she watches TV. Last week she watched 90 minutes of TV. How much reading did she do?

_____

13. When Adrian was in first grade, he joined a stamp club that sent him 5 stamps every month. If he participates in the club for 12 years, how many stamps will he have?

_____

Different Methods for Two-Digit Multiplication

Homework

Solve each multiplication problem, using any method. Use
rounding and estimation to check your work.

1. 45 × 61

_____

2. 24 × 56

_____

3. 83 × 27

_____

4. 39 × 48

_____

5. 36 × 96

_____

6. 63 × 87

_____

7. 58 × 79

_____

8. 15 × 92

_____

9. 33 × 43

_____

10. 76 × 29

_____

11. 69 × 63

_____

12. 84 × 23

_____

Remembering

Identify the property that is shown.

1. $2 \times 8 \times 5 = 2 \times 5 \times 8$

_____

2. $(9 \times 4) \times 2 = 9 \times (4 \times 2)$

_____

3. $2 \times (5 \times 9) = (2 \times 5) \times 9$

_____

4. $2(6 + 7) = 2 \times 6 + 2 \times 7$

_____

Find the perimeter and area of each figure.

5.

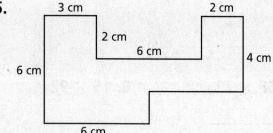

6.

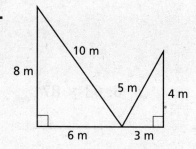

$P =$ _____ $A =$ _____ $P =$ _____ $A =$ _____

Estimate the sum or difference.

7. $236 + 451 =$ _____

8. $775 - 459 =$ _____

Solve.

Show your work.

9. Ben has 15 puzzles and 27 CDs. When he takes a trip, he likes to bring one puzzle and one CD as entertainment. How many trips can he take with a different puzzle and CD pair?

_____

10. A bike club wants to make license plates for the neighborhood bikes. Each license plate has a letter followed by a digit. How many different license plates can be made?

_____

Check Products of Two-Digit Numbers

Homework

Solve using any method and show your work. Check your work with estimation.

1. 55 × 64 _____

2. 42 × 67 _____

3. 59 × 32 _____

4. 78 × 44 _____

5. 62 × 23 _____

6. 53 × 28 _____

7. 71 × 35 _____

8. 22 × 66 _____

Solve.

Show your work.

9. Keesha walks 12 blocks to school every day. One day, she counts 88 sidewalk squares in one block. If each block has the same number of sidewalk squares, how many squares does Keesha walk on as she walks *to* and *from* school each day?

_____

10. The Card Collector's Club is having a meeting. Each member brings 25 sports cards to show and trade. If 35 members attend, how many cards do they bring altogether?

_____

11. On a separate sheet of paper, write and solve your own multiplication word problem.

Name _____ **Date** _____

Remembering

Subtract. Show your work.

1. 25,063 − 5,867   **2.** 40,000 − 18,794   **3.** 1,460,376 − 672,807

Find the perimeter and area of each figure.

4.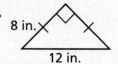

8 in.
12 in.

P = _____

A = _____

5.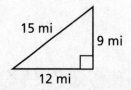

15 mi
9 mi
12 mi

P = _____

A = _____

6.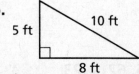

5 ft
10 ft
8 ft

P = _____

A = _____

Solve each problem, using the following information.

Rachina's family has a jar of money. Over a whole year, the family members put their change in the jar. When their vacation time comes, they use the money to have some fun together. Help Rachina's family figure out how much money they saved this year.

7. Rachina makes exactly 3 piles of 40 quarters. What is the value of all the quarters they saved?

Show your work.

_____

8. Her Uncle Jake puts the pennies in rolls. There are 50 pennies in 1 roll. He makes 26 rolls of pennies and has 16 pennies left over. How much money in pennies did their jar contain?

_____

9. Her mother counts the nickels. She makes piles of 10 nickels and comes up with 12 piles plus 6 more nickels. What is the value of all of the nickels in the jar?

_____

Practice Multiplication

Homework

Multiply, using your favorite method. Show your work.

1. 7×800

2. 58×700

3. 36×500

4. 67×800

_____ _____ _____ _____

Solve.

Show your work.

5. During her 8-week summer vacation, Jamie read an average of 3 books per week. Each book had about 40 pages. About how many pages did Jamie read over the summer?

_____

6. A female fly lays about 200 eggs at a time. If she lays eggs twice a week, about how many eggs will she lay in 4 weeks?

_____

7. The city needs to pave two sections of road. One section is 9 meters wide and 90 meters long. The other is the same width and twice as long. How many square meters of paving material do they need to do the job?

_____

8. There are 30 students in Mr. Lee's science class. For an experiment, he gives each student 8 glass tubes, 2 plastic hoses, and 12 pieces of paper. How many items does Mr. Lee give out in all to the students?

_____

Multiplication With Hundreds **169**

Find the product.

1. $36 \times 27 =$ _____

2. $42 \times 18 =$ _____

3. $71 \times 64 =$ _____

4. $53 \times 83 =$ _____

This is an overhead map of Gretchen's home and yard. Use your centimeter ruler and the map to answer the questions below.

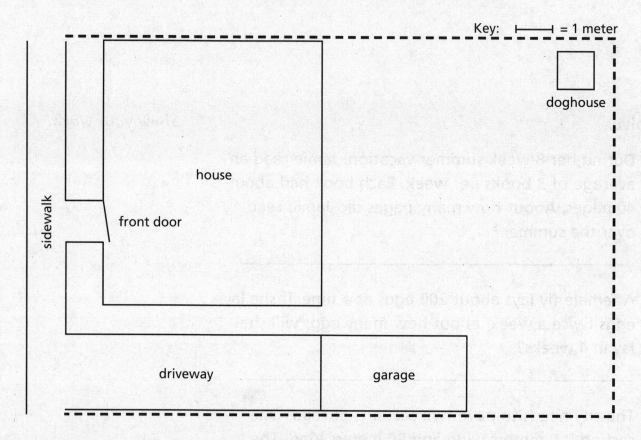

Key: ⊢————⊣ = 1 meter

doghouse

sidewalk

house

front door

driveway   garage

5. The line (— — —) that goes around 3 sides of the yard shows a fence. What is the total length of the fence?

_____

6. What is the *area* of the house? of the garage? of the doghouse? of the sidewalk, including the part in front of the door and the driveway?

_____

_____

Multiplication With Hundreds

Homework

Multiply, using your favorite method. Show each step.

1. 4 × 7,000   **2.** 29 × 3,000   **3.** 52 × 8,000   **4.** 35 × 5,000

_____   _____   _____   _____

Complete each equation.

5. 3 × 1 = _____   **6.** 1 × 3 = _____

7. 3 × 10 = _____   **8.** 10 × 3 = _____

9. 3 × 100 = _____   **10.** 100 × 3 = _____

11. 3 × 1,000 = _____   **12.** 1,000 × 3 = _____

13. 30 × 1 = _____   **14.** 1 × 30 = _____

15. 30 × 10 = _____   **16.** 10 × 30 = _____

17. 30 × 100 = _____   **18.** 100 × 30 = _____

19. 30 × 1,000 = _____   **20.** 1,000 × 30 = _____

21. Write three sentences to tell what you notice about the patterns in the numbers.

_____

_____

_____

_____

_____

Remembering

Factor each number into its prime factors.

1. 14 _____

2. 19 _____

3. 36 _____

4. 42 _____

5. 50 _____

6. 63 _____

7. 78 _____

8. 88 _____

9. 95 _____

10. Which of the numbers in exercises 1–9 is a prime number? Explain why.

_____

_____

_____

Find the area of each figure.

11.
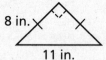

8 in.

11 in.

_____

12.
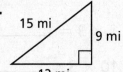

15 mi

9 mi

12 mi

_____

13.
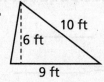

10 ft

6 ft

9 ft

_____

Solve each problem.

Show your work.

14. Mrs. Bergen is buying a 6-foot by 5-foot rug. How many square feet will the rug cover?

_____

15. Molly runs 6 lengths of a 50-yard track. How far does she run?

_____

16. Mr. Jordan is painting the side of a barn that is 50 feet wide and 60 feet high. How many square feet will he paint?

_____

Homework

1. Connections

Make a timeline to show what you did today.

2. Reasoning and Proof

Support or disprove the following statement with examples.

A right triangle cannot have an obtuse angle.

_____

_____

_____

3. Communication

Three sides of a quadrilateral measure 4 cm, 5 cm, and 9 cm. The perimeter is 24 cm. What is the length of the fourth side? How did you find the answer?

_____

_____

_____

4. Representation

Draw a figure that is not changed by a horizontal reflection or a translation.

Name _____ **Date** _____

Remembering

Find the product.

1. 24 × 53 = _____

2. 36 × 15 = _____

3. 63 × 72 = _____

4. 49 × 86 = _____

Factor each number into its prime factors.

5. 18

_____

_____

6. 64

_____

_____

7. 27

_____

_____

8. 66

_____

_____

9. 40

_____

_____

10. 72

_____

_____

11. 80

_____

_____

12. 30

_____

_____

13. 21

_____

_____

Find the area of each figure.

14.

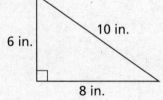

6 in.   10 in.   8 in.

_____

15.

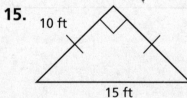

10 ft   15 ft

_____

Use Mathematical Processes

Homework

Solve the word problem.   *Show your work.*

1. A room is 5 m wide and 7 m long. What is the area
   of the floor?

   _____

2. A farm is 1 km wide and 2 km long. What is its area
   in square kilometers?

   _____

3. Write and solve two metric-area word problems.

   _____

   _____

   _____

   _____

   _____

   _____

   _____

   _____

   _____

   _____

   _____

   _____

   _____

   _____

   _____

Name _____ **Date** _____

Remembering

Write the number for the word name.

1. one thousand, forty _____

2. six thousand, thirty-seven _____

3. nine thousand, four hundred sixty-three _____

4. one hundred fifty thousand, two _____

Write the word name for the number.

5. 204 _____

6. 4,827 _____

7. 11,005 _____

8. 56,000,789 _____

Round each number to the nearest ten, hundred, and thousand.

	Ten	Hundred	Thousand
9. 1,748	_____	_____	_____
10. 50,637	_____	_____	_____
11. 739	_____	_____	_____
12. 2,009,584	_____	_____	_____

Solve.

Show your work.

13. Augusto had four cards each, measuring 3 in. by 5 in. He taped them together to make one larger card. Draw the new arrangement of cards and name its perimeter.

_____

_____

_____

Measure Area

Homework

Complete.

1. How many milliliters are equal to 3 L?

_____

2. How many milliliters are equal to 35 L?

_____

3. How many liters are equal to 5,000 milliliters?

_____

4. How many kiloliters are equal to 5,000 liters?

_____

Solve.

Show your work.

5. Every morning for breakfast, Mika drinks 200 mL of orange juice. How many liters of orange juice does she drink in 10 days?

_____

6. Steven's crayon box is 7 cm wide, 2 dm long, and 4 cm deep. What is the volume of Steven's crayon box in cubic centimeters?

_____

7. Write and solve a metric-volume word problem and a metric-capacity word problem.

_____

_____

_____

_____

_____

_____

Remembering

Use each digit once. Write the greatest number and the
least number you can make.

	Greatest	**Least**
1. 9, 4, 8, 1, 2, 4, 0, 7	_____	_____
2. 6, 4, 1, 9, 2, 1, 3, 0	_____	_____
3. 7, 0, 6, 3, 0, 5, 8	_____	_____
4. 5, 3, 7, 0, 4, 2, 6	_____	_____

Compare. Write >, <, or =.

5. 8,135 _____ 8,153   **6.** 67,280 _____ 68,720   **7.** 153,609 _____ 156,390

8. 2,409 _____ 2,904   **9.** 92,416 _____ 91,426   **10.** 502,147 _____ 520,147

11. 6,711 _____ 6,171   **12.** 89,735 _____ 83,597   **13.** 620,793 _____ 620,739

Write the value of the underlined digit.

14. 5,6̲73 _____   **15.** 19̲,357 _____   **16.** 4̲7,678 _____

17. 6̲78,924 _____   **18.** 1,83̲9,155 _____   **19.** 8,0̲84,576 _____

Solve.

Show your work.

20. Mr. Okutani is decorating a bulletin board that is
5 dm high and 7 dm wide. He has 2 packages of
border that each contain 125 cm of border. Does
he have enough border to go all around the
outside of the bulletin board? Explain.

_____

_____

_____

_____

Measure Volume and Capacity

Homework

Complete.

1. How many grams are in 4 kg? _____

2. How many grams are in 40 kg? _____

3. How many grams are in 400 kg? _____

4. How many grams are in 5,000 kg? _____

5. How many grams are in 50,000 kg? _____

6. How many grams are in 500,000 kg? _____

Solve.

Show your work.

7. Angie's puppy weighed 3 kg when she first got it. Two years later, it weighed 9 kg. How many grams of weight did the puppy gain?

_____

8. Mr. Silverstein bought 3 packages of rice at the store. The big package contained 1 kg. Each of the 2 smaller packages contained 450 grams. How many grams of rice did he buy in all?

_____

9. Write and solve two metric-mass or metric-weight word problems.

_____

_____

_____

_____

_____

_____

Remembering

Add or subtract. Round and estimate the addition or subtraction to see if your answer makes sense.

1. 37,496 + 1,530

_____

2. 165,309 + 31,284

_____

3. 488,531 − 48,260

_____

4. 195,307 + 40,682

_____

5. 514,736 + 278,093

_____

6. 694,301 − 250,682

_____

7. 6,830 + 270,915

_____

8. 5,750,813 − 41,978

_____

9. 9,835,061 − 784,255

_____

Solve.

Show your work.

10. Every year, Edith runs 5K (5 km) races each month for 6 months. The other 6 months she runs 10K races. How many kilometers does she run in races each year?

_____

11. The floor of Rachel's bedroom is 16 sq m. Reggie's bedroom is 4 m wide and 5 m long. Whose bedroom is bigger? Explain your thinking.

_____

_____

Measure Mass

Name _____ **Date** _____

This table shows average temperatures in degrees Celsius for some U.S. cities in January and July.

Use the information in the table to answer the questions.

City and State	Average Temperatures (°C)	
	January	July
Bismarck, North Dakota	−14	21
Caribou, Maine	−12	18
Fairbanks, Alaska	−25	15
Honolulu, Hawaii	22	27
Houston, Texas	11	28
Olympia, Washington	3	17
Phoenix, Arizona	11	34
St. Louis, Missouri	−2	26
San Francisco, California	9	16
Savannah, Georgia	10	27

1. Which city has the warmest average temperature in January? _____

2. Which city has the coldest average temperature in January? _____

3. Which city has the warmest average temperature in July? _____

4. Which city has the coldest average temperature in July? _____

5. Which city has the smallest variation in average temperatures between January and July? Explain.

   _____

   _____

6. Which city has the greatest variation in average temperatures between January and July? Explain.

   _____

   _____

7. On a separate sheet of paper, write and solve two word problems about the temperatures shown in the table.

Name _____ **Date** _____

Remembering

Multiply.

1. 67	2. 98	3. 35	4. 26	5. 44	6. 59
× 3	× 7	× 8	× 13	× 37	× 82

Write the metric unit that you think best measures each amount or distance. Explain your thinking.

7. the distance between two cities

_____

8. the amount of water in a glass

_____

9. the height of a building

_____

10. the width of a piece of paper

_____

Solve.

11. Melba has a 2-liter bottle of water. She and 2 friends each
drink 250 mL of the water. Together, did they drink
more than or less than half of the bottle of water?
Explain your thinking.

_____

_____

_____

12. Two bottles of apple juice cost the same amount of
money. One contains 1 L and the other contains
1,200 mL. Which bottle is the better buy?

_____

_____

_____

Measure Temperature